LESSONS FOR LIFE 1

LESSONS
FOR LIFE 1

JILL MASTERS

THE WAKEMAN TRUST, LONDON

THE WAKEMAN TRUST
(UK Registered Charity)
5 Templar Street
London SE5 9JB

LESSONS FOR LIFE 1

© Copyright 1991, Jill Masters
First printed 1991
Reprinted 1996

ISBN 1 870855 07 8

Cover design by Andrew Sides

Visual aid drawings by Alan MacGregor
with graphics and presentation by Andrew Owen

Printed in Great Britain by J. W. Arrowsmiths of Bristol.

CONTENTS
Book 1

	Page
Introduction	7
Starting or Enlarging a Sunday School	11

Series 1 – Mark's Gospel (Part I)
Miracles Demonstrating Jesus' Power — 15

Lesson	Title	
1	Jesus' Power Over Nature	17
2	Jesus' Power Over Death	21
3	Jesus' Power Over the Devil	25
4	Jesus' Power Over Need	28
5	Jesus' Power Over Illness	31

Series 2 – Genesis (Part I)
In the Beginning — 35

6	In the Beginning, God	36
7	The Creation of Life and Man	41
8	The Fall of Man	44
9	Cain and Abel	51
10	Noah	55
11	Revision of Series 1 and 2	59

Series 3 – Mark's Gospel (Part II)
Opposition to Jesus — 62

12	Prejudice	63
13	Superiority and Pride	69
14	Hardness and Hate	72
15	Hypocrisy	75
16	Dishonesty	78
17	How Can We Go to Heaven?	82

Series 4 – Acts (Part I)
Highlights from the Conversion
and Preaching Journeys of Paul   **88**

18	Saul's Conversion	92
19	The Conversion of Lydia at Philippi	97
20	The Conversion of the Jailor	100
21	Paul Visits Athens	103
22	A Riot at Ephesus	107
23	Paul Before Felix	110
24	Onesimus	114
25	Revision	117

Series 5 – Genesis (Part II)
God's Great Plans   **120**

26	God Begins a Plan with Abraham	122
27	God Tests Abraham and Reveals His Plan	126
28	Lot Experiments with His Own Plan	129
29	God's Plan for Finding Isaac's Wife	135
30	Esau Sells His Share in God's Plan	139
31	God's Plan of Grace	143
32	Jacob Becomes Israel	148
33	Joseph is Shown God's Plan in His Dreams	151
34	The Plan Unfolds – Strangely at First	157
35	The Dreams Come True	161
36	The First Plan Completed	163
37	Revision	166

Series 6 – John's Gospel
The 'I AM' Sayings of the Lord Jesus   **168**

38	The Living Water	170
39	The Bread of Life	174
40	The Light of the World	178
41	The Good Shepherd	182
42	The Resurrection and the Life	187
43	The Way, the Truth and the Life	191
44	The True Vine	196
45	The Lamb of God	199
46	The Son of God (Revision)	203

INTRODUCTION

This is the first of four volumes of Sunday School lesson notes, each covering one year of a four-year lesson plan (set out on pages 206-207). Take-home leaflets (in 'master' form for local photocopying) to accompany the lessons in this book, are also published.

Teachers may like to bear in mind that *Lessons for Life* lesson notes all have a threefold aim. First, they have an evangelistic aim, using selected Bible portions which are clearly intended for evangelistic application. Each lesson seeks to confront children with a true understanding of truths and arguments which, under the Holy Spirit, could lead to conversion.

Secondly, they are intended to give a good outline knowledge of all the Scriptures. The syllabus seeks to deal with Bible events in an orderly manner, worthy of the Word of God. The Old Testament is mainly dealt with chronologically, so that the pattern of God's dealings with mankind before Christ is known and appreciated. In this lesson scheme, the Old Testament lessons are interleaved with the Gospels and *Acts*. Both children and teachers prefer this method of following a basic historical pattern, to those approaches which jump from one part of the Bible to another with such frequency that all perspective is lost. Each week this scheme provides another instalment in the great plan of God. Pastoral needs of young believers can be catered for, so that parents (unbelievers as well as believers) will appreciate that their children are receiving a biblical education.

Thirdly, these lesson notes aim to present vital spiritual topics to the minds of the young. The plan of the Bible itself suggests various themes which should be highlighted in our teaching. For example, the early chapters of *Genesis* offer an opportunity to present a serious challenge to the whole evolutionary/atheistic outlook; the book of *Exodus* presents the pilgrimage theme; the lessons from the latter kings of the Old Testament include a number of apologetic arguments from archaeology, vindicating the Bible as the Word of God, proven and trustworthy. Luke's Gospel is divided into two series – the parables, and a catalogue of conversions entitled, 'People Who Followed Jesus'. John's Gospel lends itself to an easily remembered series on the great 'I Am' sayings of the Lord.

By this means we aim to offer the children a great and varied Gospel challenge as they set out on life's journey. Prayerfully, our concern is that it will lead them to the Saviour in early years, but if not, it will plant in their minds and hearts a knowledge of the Lord which can be used by His Spirit in later years to prick their consciences and lead them to seek the Saviour.

Many published lesson schemes provide separate notes and worksheets for each age group. *Lessons for Life* adopts a different policy. Experience has shown that teachers are the best people to adapt the lessons to each individual class. These notes therefore contain material which can be adapted to the needs of all age groups, from Beginners (pre-school age) to the teenage Bible Class. A range of suggested applications and guidelines is provided so that teachers may utilise the particular points most suited to their age group. Teachers of older classes often use the complete lesson outline, while those teaching younger classes select fewer points. In the many years this scheme has been in use in large numbers of Sunday Schools, our feedback has shown that teachers are very happy to 'grade' the lessons for themselves.

The lesson system is tailored to fit around the Sunday School year. Most Sunday Schools, like day schools, will divide their programme into three terms a year. Most will want to break off from regular lessons for Christmas, New Year, Easter and other holidays and special occasions. Speakers usually choose and prepare their own subject on these Sundays, and it is assumed, therefore, that a maximum of 46 lessons per year is required. The lessons are grouped into series, and individual Sunday Schools may use these in any order to suit their Sunday School year. However, the Old Testament series should be kept in chronological order, whereas New Testament series may be fitted into the year according to choice.

The promise of the Lord that His Word will not return to Him empty *(Isaiah 55.11)* proves a great incentive to continue through days of patient toil. Slowly and surely the satisfaction of watching God's Word taking effect in the lives and behaviour of young children confirms its truthfulness. In days of irreligion and apathy amongst the adult population, it is extremely touching to witness large numbers of children gathered together, and to see the Lord still preparing His praise out of the mouths of infants *(Matthew 21.16)*.

He who goes to and fro weeping, carrying his bag of seed, shall indeed come again with a shout of joy, bringing his sheaves with him (Psalm 126.6).

Children's Work – *Our Biblical Authority*

A Gospel charge: *Gather the people together, men, and women, and CHILDREN, and thy stranger that is within thy gates, that they may hear, and that they may learn, and fear the Lord your God, and observe to do all the words of this law: and that their children, which have not known any thing, may hear, and learn to fear the Lord your God, as long as ye live in the land . . . (Deuteronomy 31.12-13).*

Jesus said: *Take heed that ye despise not one of these little ones (Matthew 18.10).*

Whoso shall receive one such little child in my name receiveth me (Matthew 18.5).

Whoso shall offend one of these little ones which believe in me, it were better for him that a millstone were hanged about his neck, and that he were drowned in the depth of the sea (Matthew 18.6).

Suffer little children, and forbid them not, to come unto me: for of such is the kingdom of heaven (Matthew 19.14).

When the chief priests and scribes saw . . . the children crying in the temple, and saying, Hosanna to the son of David; they were sore displeased, and said unto him, Hearest thou what these say? And Jesus saith unto them, Yea; have ye never read, Out of the mouth of babes and sucklings thou hast perfected praise? (Matthew 21.15-16.)

Jesus said to Peter: *Feed my lambs (John 21.15).*

And he said unto them, Go ye into all the world, and preach the gospel to every creature (Mark 16.15). (As C. H. Spurgeon remarked concerning this verse, 'Are not children creatures?')

From the Old Testament: *And it shall come to pass, when your children shall say unto you, What mean ye by this service? that ye shall say . . . (Exodus 12.26-27).*

Train up a child in the way he should go: and when he is old, he will not depart from it (Proverbs 22.6).

And from the epistles: *Fathers . . . bring them* [your children] *up in the nurture and admonition of the Lord (Ephesians 6.4).*

Children, obey your parents in the Lord: for this is right (Ephesians 6.1).

From a child thou hast known the holy scriptures, which are able to make thee wise unto salvation through faith which is in Christ Jesus (2 Timothy 3.15).

STARTING OR ENLARGING A SUNDAY SCHOOL

Some Practical Suggestions

Understand *the importance* of representing the Lord to a new generation. Everything must be done worthily. Enlist the earnest support of the church prayer meeting.

Consider the *best time* to hold a Sunday School. In some areas a morning school seems to be the more successful arrangement. However, where possible and suitable, an afternoon Sunday School enables the whole church fellowship to give its undivided attention to the children's work, and so much larger gatherings of children are achievable. Many children from unbelieving families are pleased to have something to do each Sunday afternoon, and parents are glad to send them. Often the morning Sunday School, arranged to fit in before the morning service, is too early for unbelieving families; nevertheless local considerations may demand it.

The opening day. Make every effort to start with as large a number of children as you can manage. A crowd draws a crowd. Children do not respect small, pathetic gatherings. (Better to meet in a small, crowded room than a large empty hall.)

Gathering the children. (a) Enthuse other church members to send their own families, neighbours' children and friends. (b) Visit the neighbourhood with well-presented invitation cards or letters a week or two beforehand. (c) Make personal visits to the homes during the previous week to answer queries, press home the invitation and encourage the children to come. (d) Provide a team of adults who will call for the children on the day. (e) Arrange for as many cars, minibuses, etc, as possible to collect the children – especially from further-away places. If Sunday School is held in the afternoon almost every car-owning member of the fellowship can be asked to join the team. (f) This team of callers and collectors will build up an invaluable link with the families, providing Gospel opportunities in the neighbourhood which would take years to build without the tie of children.

Registration. Organise an effective registration system. It is best if this is undertaken by a person (or team) not involved in teaching, so that they can give it their full concentration. Plan a reward system for regular attendance and good behaviour. Children respond to the smallest incentive – and they love novelty. Small prizes, new goals and fresh charts work wonders, and are in keeping with the heavenly principle of rewards and punishments.

A supply of printed cards bearing a photograph or drawing of the church premises with title and address etc, will set parents' minds at rest should they fear their children are attending a cult meeting. Each new child could be issued with such a card and asked to fill in details of their age, address, telephone number, etc. The Registrar should enable the Sunday School personnel to arrange a thorough plan for visiting absentees. Children are fickle and will need to be reminded to come. There are many other attractions on Sunday!

Presentation and Visual Aids. Ensure a supply of well-presented hymn-sheets, chorus-sheets, team charts, etc, so that the children will be favourably impressed by the general atmosphere. It is important that the standard of presentation of visual aids should be as high as the children would expect from their day school. Anything less dishonours the Lord. Teachers should make use of felt-tip pens, letraset and photocopiers to help them produce attractive visual aids.

The visual aids suggested throughout this book involve a

certain degree of drawing skill. If teachers cannot reproduce these pictures themselves or with artistic help from within their fellowship, they will nevertheless find the words employed very helpful in the presenting of the lesson. Use large pieces of card and write the visual aid words with a thick felt-tip marker.

Hymns and music. Give this matter careful thought. We have to show our children that we worship a holy God and that to be a Christian is to be separate from this sinful, carnal world. Down the centuries and around the world, Christians have had to leave behind the worldly culture of their day and provide music and praise worthy of the Lord.

There is a heritage of short, simple, theologically rich and feelingful hymns and choruses written by Christians who dedicated themselves to Gospel work among children in past years. There are also many memorable and tuneful melodies available for our use. Sadly, much of this Gospel-rich material has been discarded as old-fashioned by the pop-music generation, and children have been taught shallow sentiments to fit modern rhythms.

Many older hymns convey the whole Gospel message to the lost in the most simple language. If children learn these verses while young they will remember the words through life and take the Gospel challenge to their deathbeds. Long after their Sunday School days are forgotten, this message of the Lord's redeeming love will stay with them. Therefore we ought to give serious attention to the hymns we teach and the music we use.

Check List for Teachers Preparing a Lesson

Read the Bible passage carefully: the lesson notes are not a substitute.

Check the genuineness of your personal concern for your class. Children will quickly spot a hypocritical or indifferent spirit.

Prepare some form of visual aid for the lesson, either of the kind suggested in these notes, or at least provide relevant news or magazine pictures, or objects which will illustrate the points made.

Consider how to introduce the lesson. An interesting

introduction is vital to arrest the children's attention from the start.

Once the class is listening, maintain an interesting, absorbing presentation throughout the lesson. Do not break attention by stopping for questions or 'chat' in mid lesson. (Questions can be asked at the end of the lesson.)

Make your own notes with headings. Even if you are unable to refer to these during the lesson, the notes will help fix the essential form of the lesson in your mind and so give you liberty and fluency.

Examine your lesson content. Does your lesson help the children see some aspect of the reality and horror of sin? Does your lesson contain a 'gracious' aspect: will it include some real effort to convince them of God's kindness and mercy in making a way of forgiveness at Calvary? How will the lesson end? The wording of the closing 'appeal' should be prepared with care. Never think that this is basic and therefore easy; this important part of the lesson always needs to be fresh and compelling.

Ask the Lord's blessing on every part of your labours, remembering His words: *I am the vine, you are the branches; he who abides in Me, and I in him, he bears much fruit:* FOR APART FROM ME YOU CAN DO NOTHING *(John 15.5).*

Series 1
Mark's Gospel (Part I)
Miracles Demonstrating
JESUS' POWER

Introduction to Mark's Gospel. Mark's Gospel is divided into three sections, the first two of which appear in this book. They are entitled:–

I – Jesus' Power – Five lessons on the miracles and what they teach us.

II – Opposition to Jesus – Incidents which show the bitter hostility which confronted the Saviour. Warnings on how to avoid such fatal attitudes ourselves.

III – Gains and Losses in Following Jesus – Examples and teaching from the Gospel narrative, challenging us to give this matter serious consideration.

Lessons on Jesus' Power

1 – Jesus' Power Over Nature

'Who, then, is this, that even the wind and sea obey Him?' asked the shaken witnesses of this amazing event. Unique in the history of this world, this great miracle should set us thinking too.

2 – Jesus' Power Over Death

Since the birth of civilisation man has pitted his wits against death. Individuals and communities have had very little success in their quest to delay or prevent death. Today we learn of a Man Who in a moment, at a word, could command death to give up its victim with instant success. This same Jesus waits to rescue us from spiritual death.

3 – Jesus' Power Over the Devil

A man tormented and invaded by the devil seemed a hopeless case, but once again Jesus' power was effective and his release immediate. We are all enslaved to some degree by the enemy of our souls, and Jesus alone can set us free.

4 – Jesus' Power Over Need

Every one of us is involved in the lifelong struggle for money and the supply of basic necessities. The crowd were quick to grasp the significance of this unique and amazing event. But instead of allowing it to unveil the person and power of the Lord they squandered it on selfish greed and gain. What are our motives for seeking Him?

5 – Jesus' Power Over Illness

Even the youngest children have experienced some physical ailments, enough to make them sensitive to those who suffer gravely. The Saviour was able to bring relief to those who bore all kinds of disease and disablement. Immediate and complete restoration came to many people at His command. He has the same authority to cure us of the disease of sin. Have we ever applied to Him for a cure?

Teachers' Introduction to the Series

Most children have at least a slight knowledge of these miracles. Sadly, many regard them as being in the same category as fairy tales. To them they belong in the land of make-believe and fiction. Our first aim therefore will be to convince the class that we are dealing with history and fact, and not with idle tales. Viewed in this light, these events are staggering and amazing. They impress upon the mind the divine power of the Lord. We must aim to have the children asking with the disciples, 'Who, then, is this?'

Signs. We are told in *John 20.30-31* that the miracles were 'signs'. They teach us not only Who the Lord is, but how He works. Our forebears regarded them as 'acted parables' – signs of what His love and power can do spiritually. This thought will add a new dimension to the lesson. Children who consider that they already know these events can be shown that there is a whole new layer of meaning for them to discover which will challenge and affect them in a very personal way.

Visual Aid

VA 1 (see page 18) is designed for use throughout this series.

Jesus' Power Over Nature (1)
The Stilling of the Storm

Mark 4.35-41

Aim: To show the children why they should trust the Lord, and how they may trust Him.

Lesson Outline

Alert the children to the enormous significance of this unique and staggering event. Talk to them about the use of signs and signals in everyday life. Pressing a sign or key on a computer provides a whole mass of information. Out in the countryside a single name on a signpost may signal a great change in the scenery as we enter a vast town. Explain that when the Lord Jesus did one of His mighty miracles it too was a sign to inform about great and important things. The way in which Jesus calmed the storm on the Sea of Galilee was such a sign.

Sign A – The journey begins. Describe how Jesus Himself made the suggestion that He and the disciples should cross the sea. Other vessels followed and became involved in all that happened.

Life itself is like a great voyage on an unpredictable sea. We set out as inexperienced sailors. Do we laugh at the need for a chart, compass and pilot? Is the Lord with us?

Sign B – A vulnerable craft. As the disciples stood on the shore their boat looked strong and reliable, but once the storm blew up it was tossed about like a matchbox, so that they feared it would be crushed by the waves. We travel across life's sea in a frail craft. We may imagine that our bodies are healthy and strong, but really there is only a

Cut a five pointed star out of thick paper. Fold points into centre. Write "JESUS' POWER OVER"... on folded-in points. Open the star points and draw the pictures below on the inside, or glue in photos from magazines etc.

Open as lessons proceed.

VA 1 – *Visual Aid for use with lessons on 'Jesus' Power'.*

heartbeat between us and death, and the forces we shall meet are much more powerful than we are.

Sign C – Danger! Describe how suddenly a small cloud appeared in the evening sky, the wind blew up and within a short time the tranquil evening sea was transformed into a raging mass. Even these experienced fishermen were terrified. The journey of life is more dangerous than most people realise.

Ask the children if they have ever been really afraid. Help them to imagine what it feels like to be in an airliner which is diving out of control. Remind the class that life's storms bring unexpected fears and alarms which often take away our happiness and determine what we do. At one moment we are looking forward to, say, a holiday, or a new toy or gadget, when all of a sudden disaster strikes. Perhaps unemployment hits the family or a terrible quarrel tears the family apart, or it may be that a parent becomes very ill. Could we cope? As we grow through youth will we stand up to sin and temptation, or will we be terrified of the scorn of those who yield to it – and join them? Life is full of such fears and alarms.

Sign D – Testing our trust. The disciples thought they were following the Lord, but He put them to the test by staying asleep during the terrifying storm. Did they believe in Him? Did they truly trust that, asleep or awake, He was the Lord, and therefore they would be safe? On dry land they thought that they trusted Him, but now He caused their faith to be put to the test. No one is really converted without *trusting* Christ.

Sign E – Jesus' mighty power. Human beings do not easily understand the spiritual power of the Lord Jesus. The disciples, experienced seamen as they were, panicked. Even though Jesus was on board, they were certain that they were about to die! In their state of desperation they showed that they did not think that Jesus could save them if He was asleep! Like any ordinary man, He must be awake in order to do anything to help them! If they had really appreciated that He was God, they would have realised that He could not drown in an accident.

Are we any better? Have we realised that the Lord Jesus,

though He is now out of our sight in Heaven, has the spiritual power to change our inner hearts with just a glance? He can change our character, enable us to understand the Gospel, strengthen and bless us without being physically present.

Sign F – His power towards us. The Lord's will is all-powerful, even over seemingly uncontrollable things. Just as He commands the sea, He can transform the most rebellious person and bring that person to know and love Him. When we pray to Him for help, even though we have sinned against Him, He will immediately come to our aid and save us with a word.

We have heard of others who claim to be able to heal people, but no one has ever pretended to be able to control the weather. Yet the Lord Jesus, in the presence of many wide-awake men, said only three words to the waves and the sea, and the effect was immediate. Even in an age of satellites, spacecraft, weather computers, etc, we cannot predict the weather with certainty, let alone control it with words.

Tell the children how the Lord has utterly changed not only the weather – but also the lives of millions of people. Also He has revealed His great power to them day by day, answering their prayers and helping them, particularly in their service and work for Him. Remind the children that the Lord Jesus has not changed. He is still Lord of the universe and Sovereign of all.

Sign G – Our sinful unbelief. The Lord will rebuke the failure of all who refuse to trust Him. Tell how Jesus voiced His disappointment to His disciples. The wind and the sea 'knew' and obeyed their Creator, yet His own disciples had panicked and behaved as if He were nothing more than a helpless human being. (Compare with *Isaiah 1.3*.)

Close the lesson by showing the class how it is possible for us to grieve the Lord by refusing to believe in Him. He came from the courts of Heaven to do the greatest miracle of all – to die on the Cross so that He might have the right and the power to save many, many children and adults from their sin.

How tragic when we turn away from the Saviour and put our trust in anything or anyone beside! Encourage the children to look at the evidence and stare in wonder and amazement at the Son of God – Ruler of the sea – Who came to this world to rescue all those who, realising that they will perish without Him, call out to Him for help.

Jesus' Power Over Death (2)
Jairus' Daughter

Mark 5.21-43

Aim: To show the children why they need new life from the Saviour and how they can obtain it. (Please note that this lesson is taught out of chronological order to achieve a better topical sequence.)

Lesson Outline

Describe the crowds which met Jesus as He returned to their side of the sea. Among them was a man many people recognised – Jairus, a ruler of the synagogue. Tell how Jairus, though a ruler himself, fell at Jesus' feet, and pleaded with Him earnestly.

How should I come to Jesus? Show how God's Word is not just a story-book, but a book which speaks to us and challenges us today. Even these few words show us the way to come to Jesus. Do we imagine that becoming a Christian is a light-hearted affair, like joining a club? Is it something we can do one day and forget the next? Do we think that Jesus is desperate for followers and will therefore accept anyone in whatever mood they come?

Contrast this modern attitude with that of Jairus:

(1) He came humbly. He knelt. He knew he did not deserve the attention and help of Jesus. Many religious rulers had been critical of the Saviour; perhaps at one time Jairus had been one of them.

(2) He came in a spirit of desperation. He begged and pleaded very earnestly with Jesus to come – no one else could save his daughter. As ruler of the synagogue he would have tried all the doctors and cures in town, but none had been able to help.

(3) He came – and he persisted. When Jesus turned aside to help a woman in the crowd, he did not give up. He stood by, trusting, hoping, waiting, until Jesus came to see his daughter.

Similarly we must come to Jesus recognising that He is Lord of all, that we do not deserve and cannot earn His attention. In fact, we need His mercy because of how we have always treated Him in the past. Like Jairus we must also realise how much we need Him. He is the only One Who can rescue us from sin and death. Unless He converts us we will be eternally lost. Finally, we must show Jesus that we are in earnest. We must go on praying, asking Him to bless us. If He does not seem to answer our prayers at first, we must persist, showing Him that we really mean what we say and that we truly want to be converted.

Why did Jairus need Jesus? Children will identify with the answer. They will remember his daughter's age, and that she was very ill. Whether her illness was a progressively weakening disease like leukaemia, or whether the once cheerful twelve-year-old had been struck down by one of the common Eastern fevers of those days, the children will understand the great need which had come to this family.

Why the delay? Here is an issue which will stimulate the thought and interest of the children. Help them to imagine Jairus' concern as Jesus stopped to help someone else. Even more, let them picture the girl's mother at home, watching her daughter growing weaker every moment and finally slipping away into death. All was lost. Nothing could be done now; her daughter was dead. She must send messengers to fetch her husband home.

Why did Jesus allow their daughter to die? Make two suggestions: (a) Jesus was going to do something even more marvellous than Jairus had asked. (b) By restoring life to a dead girl Jesus was going to prove to Jairus, and to us, that if we trust Him, nothing is too hard for Him.

Encourage the class to notice the kindness of Jesus. He must have known what it meant for Jairus to see his servants approaching with the words he dreaded to hear: 'Your daughter is dead.' Immediately Jesus turned from everything else and told Jairus not to be afraid, but to believe. What was

Jairus to believe? He was to believe in the divine identity and power of the Lord Jesus. He was to trust Jesus with all his heart. If only we would do the same! This is the only attitude to have when we pray for conversion.

The scornful mourners. Describe the noisy scene which confronted Jesus and His small party as they reached the house, and the cries of scorn and derision as Jesus told the crowd that the girl was not dead but asleep.

Why did Jesus say that? Here is another question to provoke interest and thought.

(a) The statement of Jesus confirmed (to those who understood His use of the word *sleep*) that the little girl was dead. Many people had seen her lifeless corpse. Let the class be quite certain that Jesus raised Jairus' daughter from the dead.

(b) On the other hand, the Lord's statement showed how Jesus looks at death. Because He has power over death and can take the soul to Heaven (or send it to hell) He calls 'death' a 'sleep'. Men and women do not like to talk about death. They dread it, and hide it away. But if a person believes and knows the Lord, death for that person is really no different from going to sleep, because as soon as the body dies, the soul awakens in the presence of the Saviour.

Jesus restores life. Invite the class into the bedroom where Jairus' daughter lay. What a sad scene! A death at the age of twelve must be particularly tragic. But describe how the Lord Jesus took the girl's hand and used a tender and affectionate phrase, 'Talitha cumi.' Immediately the girl not only revived but was out of bed and walking. Probably she wondered why her family looked so surprised and amazed to see her, and she was grateful that the Lord Jesus realised how hungry she was.

What does this miracle teach us? Teachers can draw the similarities between Jairus' daughter and ourselves:–

(a) Here was just a girl, her name unknown, of no great importance outside her family, and yet the Lord of Glory came to her house to give her life from the dead.

We too may be unimportant to the world at large, but our

souls are greatly loved by the Saviour, Who was willing to give His life for sinners like us. God's mercy comes to us no matter who we may be, and no matter how low we may have fallen, so great is the wonderful mercy of God.

(b) She was dead, and the Bible tells us that we too are dead in *trespasses and sins*. We need the Saviour to take away our sins and to give us eternal life so that we can know Him and walk with Him.

(c) Many laughed and scoffed at Jesus when He held out hope for her recovery. Similarly today, many of our friends will scorn and ridicule us for believing in Him and trusting in Him to convert us.

(d) In the privacy of her room, Jesus *immediately* gave life to this young girl, and He will do the same for us when we repent of our sin and turn to Him.

Encourage those who are in earnest in your class to find a quiet place where they can speak to the Lord. They can tell Him that they are not Christians and cannot make themselves into Christians. They must ask Him to bring their souls to life. And if they really mean this, and believe in what the Lord did on Calvary to take away sin, then they will soon know and feel that He has touched their hearts and minds, and has given them a new life. The Lord will make Himself real to them.

(e) Conversion must involve our trust and belief. In that awful moment when Jairus heard that his daughter was dead, only one thought would enable him to listen to Jesus – the realisation that He really was the Lord God! Once Jairus truly believed in His identity as the Creator and eternal, all-powerful Saviour, he could trust Him fully.

Closing Plea. Close the lesson by urging the class to remember this event is history and fact – not a story. Warn them never to take it for granted because it is familiar to them. Let it remind them of Jesus' amazing power even over death, proving that He is the Son of God, and the One Who they must trust in for salvation.

Jesus' Power Over the Devil (3)
The Man of Gadara

Mark 5.1-21

Aim: To show that Jesus went out of His way to rescue and transform this most desperate case. To teach the children about the forces within us which struggle to keep us away from Christ.

Lesson Outline

A hopeless case. Taking care not to frighten younger children, tell the class how wild this demon-possessed man had become. Explain that he was worse than a madman – for he had been taken over by evil spirits who lived within him. Tell how no one could either console, help, tame, or physically overpower this poor, demented person. Everyone was terrified of him and kept well away.

Only the Lord Jesus with all His kindness and care could transform this man. Once Jesus had healed him, He returned immediately to the other shore, a fact which shows that He made this journey with this man particularly in mind.

Explain how the Saviour never changes. He came down from Heaven especially to seek and save those who are lost. He knows and loves each one of those who trust in Him, and consciously bore the punishment of all their sins. Just as He once arrived on the shores of Gadara to rescue this particular man, so He comes to call us, individually, to follow Him.

Torn in two. Describe how the demoniac responded to Jesus' arrival. It was as though half of him, his *real* self, recognised that his Deliverer had come. Even while the Lord was a long way off, he ran towards Him and fell down before Him.

Yet the other half of him, the unclean spirits who possessed him, violently reacted to the coming of the Saviour. They recognised Jesus as God's Son and they hated Him. They knew that the days of their evil possession of this man were over, and begged that, rather than be sent elsewhere, they might escape into a herd of pigs nearby. Jesus commanded them to do so.

The result. Describe the wonderful and dramatic transformation which came about. The half-naked creature who had terrified the local people as he howled and screamed amongst the tombs, was soon to be seen sitting calmly, fully clothed and in his right mind, speaking to Jesus. The man who could not be tied down, even with chains, was humbly volunteering to serve the Lord. What can this teach us?

(1) **No one is too bad for Jesus.** Tell the class that you never want to hear any of them say that they are too bad or too hopeless to come to Jesus. If He could heal this man who was so filled with evil that 2,000 pigs rushed into the sea as soon as the devils entered them, then how much more can He save any one of us?

(2) **No one need be too dominated by sin to find the Lord.** Encourage those in the class who sometimes feel that they want to turn to Jesus but are prevented because something more powerful seems to control them. It may be their sinful habits, their pride, or their excessive love for things in this world (entertainments, possessions, etc). All these things pull in the other direction and prevent them from seeking help and salvation. Show how this wild man's evil spirits could not stop him from throwing himself at Jesus' feet, even if the words which came out were the words of demons. Part of him appealed to the Lord. Part of him expressed his helplessness and desire.

If only we would take to Jesus a genuine, heartfelt appeal for forgiveness and help – and mean it – then the Saviour would curb the controlling power of our sins. Tell the children to go to Jesus just as they are – He must save, and He alone. Explain the verses –

> *Just as I am – without one plea,*
> *But that Thy blood was shed for me,*
> *And that Thou bidd'st me come to Thee,*
> *   O Lamb of God, I come.*
>
> *Just as I am – and waiting not*
> *To rid my soul of one dark blot,*
> *To Thee, Whose blood can cleanse each spot,*
> *   O Lamb of God, I come.*

Just as I am – though tossed about,
With many a conflict, many a doubt,
Fightings and fears, within, without,
*   O Lamb of God, I come.*

(3) **Nothing is too hard for Jesus.** Remind the children that problems which are far beyond man's control are easy for the Saviour to deal with – as this lesson teaches. For centuries people have investigated and campaigned for an end to all the wrong in this world – but to no effect. Human life gets no better. There are more and bigger wars than ever; famine and deprivation covers more of the world than ever before; in our own country marriage and family problems grow worse, and crime becomes steadily more organised and violent. Society's efforts to change for the better have proved pitiful.

But all those who have humbly turned to the Saviour know that He has taken away their selfish, greedy hearts and replaced them with hearts which love Him and long to please Him. Explain that most of the good things which have been established in this sin-sick world (eg: hospitals, schools) have been initiated by Christians whose chief desire was to please the Lord.

Go and tell! Close the lesson on this favourite theme. The healed man begged Jesus that he might stay with Him, such was his love for the Lord. But much as the man would have liked to stay with Jesus, the Lord asked him to do something for Him. Jesus told him that he must stay with his own people and tell them how much the Lord had done for him. In this way others also might come to believe in the Saviour and find His forgiveness.

The Lord asks us too, when we are converted, to go into all the world and take the Gospel to others who are in great need of it. If we really love Him, it will give us the greatest pleasure to obey this great command and say to others –

Come and rejoice with me!
I, once so sick at heart,
Have met with One Who knows my case,
And knows the healing art.

Come and rejoice with me!
For I have found a Friend
Who knows my heart's most secret depths
Yet loves me without end.

Jesus' Power Over Need (4)
The Feeding of the Five Thousand

Mark 6.31-44; John 6.1-15 and 66

Aim: To show how much the Saviour can do for all those children who follow Him for the right reasons.

Teachers' Introduction

As workers amongst the young, we notice how frequently the Bible refers to the place and role of children in the Lord's scheme of salvation. In John's record of this great miracle he includes the fact that the five loaves and two fish came from 'a lad' in the crowd. No one suggests that the Lord or His disciples took the boy's lunch against his will, and so we can safely assume that he gave his lunch as a willing response to all that he had heard and seen in the Saviour.

This enables us to approach the event from an unusual but particularly fitting angle. The 'lads' in the Bible Class down to the children in the Beginners Class will all identify with this boy, and this will encourage them to respond to the Lord as he did.

Lesson Outline

Set the scene for this miracle by focusing attention on the boy in John's account. Help the class to picture him, rising early, wanting to join the great crowds who were following Jesus. Emphasise the importance which boys usually attach to food. He made sure that he had a good packed lunch with him – the usual rolls, and two fish, possibly caught by his father from the nearby lake.

Jesus gone! Describe the disappointment – and in some cases annoyance – of the crowd as they discovered that Jesus was not in His usual place. Express their frustration as they discovered that He had set sail for a quiet place on the other side of the lake.

The disciples had been so busy recently that they had hardly had time even to eat properly, and so Jesus had suggested that they should get away for a day to rest on their own. However, many people were determined to hear Him teach and see His miracles. When they saw the disciples' boat moving away, they decided to run around the lake and reach the other side ahead of Jesus. Perhaps the boy was one of the first to complete the distance. Certainly by the time Jesus and the disciples arrived, a large crowd was already assembling to hear Him.

Jesus' dilemma. Ask the class what Jesus did. Did He send the crowd away, or tell them to come back another day so that He and the disciples could have their much needed rest?

Ask the children why Jesus refused to send them away. He saw their great need. He saw them like a great flock of sheep ready to be led away from God by Satan; ready to be tempted by all the thrills and novelties of this world, and not able to see the eternal dangers to which they were heading. Jesus saw the urgent need to teach the people. He wanted to show them how He could save them from their sins. No one else could teach them these things and so, instead of turning them away, He began to speak to them.

The eye of faith. Suggest that the lad we are considering listened and watched in a sympathetic manner. It is probable that he was at the very front of the crowd as he was so easily noticed by the disciples. He was certainly the only person who had come prepared to spend a long day with the Lord! So perhaps, unlike so many of the adults, this boy took to heart what he heard and saw. When he saw men and women – some deaf, blind and seriously ill – being healed he perhaps realised that Jesus must be God's Son. Who else could perform so many amazing miracles?

Hunger. Describe how the day had passed and suddenly everyone began to realise how hungry they were. The disciples suggested that the crowds should be sent away to get themselves food, but the Lord Jesus did not want to do this. He knew that many had a long journey to make on foot before they could get home and He wanted to give them something to eat before they went.

Describe the disciples' incredulity. Why, they would need the equivalent of thousands of pounds to feed such a vast crowd! (Philip complained that a sum having a present-day spending power of £3-4,000 would barely provide a meagre amount for each person!)

Possible solutions. They seemed to have forgotten that the Lord Who makes tiny seeds grow into wheat and supplies bread for the world was beside them.

Did Jesus do some amazing miracle and, with a clap of thunder, call down bread from Heaven for the great crowd? Jesus did not work that way. He worked great miracles to help people believe – not to excite and impress. Often He used the most humble means to work His greatest triumphs.

Giving away his lunch. Jesus asked for the lad's loaves and fishes. Perhaps the disciples were a little doubtful about this. What good would such a tiny amount of food be when over five thousand needed to be fed? Remind the class how Jesus once told the disciples that a widow's last penny was much more valued and useful to the Lord than a rich man's token cheque (*Mark 12.41-44*). The boy's lunch was small, but it showed how the Lord takes the seemingly small efforts of His servants (though big to them) and greatly magnifies their usefulness. True believers can be a powerful influence in the hands of the Lord.

The way Jesus works. Describe how Jesus used the lad's lunch to satisfy the huge crowd. Ask the children how much was left over.

The Lord still works in the same way. Encourage young believers by reminding them that their every effort for the Lord can be greatly blessed and multiplied by Jesus to help needy souls. Warn the class against the attitude of the vast majority of that crowd who saw the miracle with eyes of greed, and not faith. They saw the possibility of Jesus supplying their earthly needs – free food at a word! But when He spoke of heavenly bread they lost interest and deserted Him (*John 6.66*).

Urge the children not to come to Sunday School just for the fun of an afternoon out, or just to win prizes and hear interesting things. Encourage them to seek the Saviour, to allow His words to trouble them and make them seek the eternal gifts which He has come to bestow on all who see their need.

Jesus' Power Over Illness (5)
Blind Bartimaeus

Mark 10.46-52

Aim: To show how we must begin to 'see' things about Christ which we never realised before, and also to show what an amazing experience conversion is.

Lesson Outline

Help the children to respect the power of the Lord Jesus Christ by showing them a picture (or giving a vivid description) of the signboard of a modern, busy hospital. List the numerous departments.

Picture the people who today wait in long queues to undergo endless tests and then, eventually, to be treated for their problem. Then picture the crowds who were able to go to Jesus to be cured – without any tests – in a split second; at a word! He was the Son of God, Who made and designed the complexities of the human body, and Who could therefore cure all problems instantly, certainly and completely.

Explain also that if a doctor in our day possessed only a fraction of the power of Jesus to heal, he would become world-famous and fabulously rich in no time. Yet on many occasions the Lord Jesus commanded His patients not to tell anyone about their healings, and He certainly never took any money for His services.

The Lord performed His mighty miracles partly out of pity for the sufferers, but chiefly to encourage all of us to put our trust in Him as Lord and Saviour. Out of the many thousands who were cured by Jesus we turn to just one man, a blind man, to discover the kind of spiritual message which Jesus' healing conveys.

Blind Bartimaeus. Help the class to consider the handicap and deprivation of being blind. List the things blind people are not able to do, all the extra fears they experience, and the things for which they depend on other people. Explain that in addition to these trials, in the past they often had to resort to begging for their survival. Before the days of braille writing, guide-dogs and special training schemes, blind people could not perform paid jobs. So they were forced to depend on other people's pity. Wherever a crowd gathered – at the market places or sporting events – blind people would always be seen with their begging bowls.

He 'saw' Jesus. Introduce the class to Bartimaeus who lived in Jericho. Suggest ways in which he may have heard of Jesus and His many miracles. Perhaps he had joined the outskirts of a crowd one day hoping to be given money, only to hear the distant voice of Jesus. Though blind, Bartimaeus appreciated something which many sighted people 'closed their eyes' to – the fact that Jesus of Nazareth was the promised Son of David, the Messiah and Saviour. He listened to the talk about His miracles of healing and became all the more convinced. He became certain that Jesus had power to do all things. Perhaps He would give him his sight.

Ask the class into which category they fall. Are they like the crowds who followed Jesus, able to see Him, yet blind to Who He was and what He had come to do? *(Isaiah 6.9; Acts 28.26)*. Or are they like the poor beggar who could not see with his eyes, but listened and saw with his mind, so that he believed with all his heart that Jesus could save and cure him?

Jesus is passing by. Imagine Bartimaeus' anticipation as he heard a large crowd approaching. Crowds were always good news to a beggar, but he became tremendously excited when he heard that Jesus was passing by. His opportunity had come. He believed Jesus was God's Son; he knew He could heal him. All that remained was for him to call out and ask Jesus for help. There was no doubt in his mind that if only he could get to Jesus, He would heal him.

However, Bartimaeus had problems. He could not see, so he could not walk up to Jesus, especially through such a large crowd. Also, he had no friends to help him. So he began to shout. Immediately the people told him to stop, but he would not be put off.

He could not use his eyes, but he could use his voice, and

so he shouted even more loudly, *'Jesus, Son of David, have mercy on me!'* His 'prayer' was short but it said all that was necessary.

Lessons for us. By now, in this series, the children will be familiar with the way in which these miracles show how they can seek the Saviour. Several applications may be drawn from these events:–

(1) Bartimaeus welcomed Jesus' coming – do we? Perhaps we only came to Sunday School out of curiosity, to please our parents or to be with our friends, but on coming we found ourselves confronted with the Saviour of the world. We have heard His words read from the Bible, and learned what it means to be a real Christian.

We have listened to the Lord calling to young people. Are we glad like Bartimaeus? Do we realise that this is the greatest opportunity we shall ever have – that we have heard of the only Person Who can forgive our sins and take us to Heaven?

(2) Bartimaeus was not easily put off. Are we? (a) Are we put off by our weaknesses? Do we allow some little doubt or problem or some other Sunday arrangement to stand in our way? (b) Are we put off by our friends and family when they want to stop us becoming serious Christians? Bartimaeus took no notice of those who tried to silence his cries and soon they were offering him encouragement instead (v 49). If at first others scorn you for seeking Jesus, keep on! It may well be that they, too, will be seeking Him before long.

Jesus stopped. Imagine what this meant to Bartimaeus. With a vast crowd following Him, Jesus stopped for a poor blind beggar who had nothing at all to offer Him. Encourage your class by reminding them that although we are in the same position – poor, lost sinners with nothing to offer the Lord – yet He came to die for each one of those who trust Him and call out for His mercy.

'What do you want?' What amazing words to hear from the Lord of the universe, the Creator of Heaven and earth! – *What do you want Me to do for you?* Did Bartimaeus' mind begin to dream of all the things he wanted – money, a big house, etc? No, he remained single-minded. He wanted his sight and that was all he asked. Urge the children to seek the one blessing that matters – the ability to see the things of God, and have His forgiveness.

Receiving his sight. Once again we notice that the Lord Jesus did not do this miracle to gain more popularity and fame. He did not act like a magician or some vaunted faith-healer, creating an atmosphere and building up to a climax of attention before healing the man. Instead He spoke kindly to Bartimaeus and gave him his sight.

This blind man must have been overwhelmed to open his eyes for the first time and see the Lord Jesus. How wonderful to see Him! Remind all believers that in Heaven they too will see Jesus as He is and be like Him. Testify to those doubters in your class that becoming a Christian is just as wonderful an experience as a blind man receiving his sight for the first time. Explain why this is so.

He followed Jesus. Close with a note of gentle Gospel irony. Jesus told Bartimaeus to go on his way. He was now free – he could choose where to go for the first time. He no longer needed helpers to lead him. He no longer had to keep to old, familiar ways. But Mark tells us that on this first great moment of freedom he chose to follow Jesus. Explain that this too is a picture of what happens to all Christians. The Lord Jesus saves them from sin and sets them free, but immediately they gladly and freely choose to follow in His way, wherever He may lead.

> *He drew me with the cords of love,*
> *And thus He bound me to Him.*

Set free from sin, Christians testify that they willingly become slaves and servants of the Lord Jesus Christ Who loved them and gave Himself for them.

Bind us together Lord
Bind us together
With cords that cannot be broken.
Bind us together Lord
Bind us together
Bind us together with love

Series 2
Genesis (Part I)
IN THE BEGINNING

6 – In the Beginning, God
How was the earth made? How did the universe come into being? The Bible has a careful, detailed answer to these questions. It tells us we have a great Creator. Do we acknowledge Him as we should?

7 – The Creation of Life and Man
Who designed the intricacies of nature? How was man made? The only satisfactory answer to these questions is to be found in the early chapters of *Genesis*. Do we recognise that life is a gift from God and that we are responsible to Him for the way we use it?

8 – The Fall of Man
This account of the sin and rebellion of Adam and Eve summarises our own state of enmity with God. Do we appreciate the lovingkindness of the Lord in providing a way of reconciliation?

9 – Cain and Abel
Living independently of God, Cain proudly thought a gift of his own achievements should please the Lord. When God showed him that this was utterly inadequate, the enraged Cain killed his own brother, leading to a miserable existence away from God's blessing. So today, all sin and unhappiness

is due to our proud independence from our Maker.

10 – Noah

The Lord was sorry that He had made man. When God looks into our lives does He feel the same regret? He made a way of escape for Noah from the terrible judgement which follows sin, and later the Lord Jesus came to save all who heed the warning.

11 – Revision of Series 1 and 2

This revision lesson is an opportunity to draw together the great 'arguments' of both series of lessons, and to remind the children that by His mighty miracles the Lord Jesus Christ is proved to be the Son of God Who was present at the creation of the world. It is He Who is willing and able to be their Saviour.

In the Beginning, God (6)

Genesis 1.1-8; Isaiah 40.10-31

Aim: To give the Bible's own explanation of creation. To help the children understand and appreciate the great power and kindness of their Maker and to urge them to respect and love Him as they should.

Teachers' Introduction

Much of this lesson will deal with the subject of God rather than that of creation. Many have rejected the account of creation in *Genesis* because they have limited God to man-sized proportions and power. Adults who have voluntarily accepted rationalistic teaching (ie: no God) have no excuse for this. They have deliberately despised the Lord. But we can sympathise with children brought up in an atheistic atmosphere if they have an inadequate view of God.

It will be our aim in this lesson to show them the greatness, majesty and power of the Lord which was at work right at the beginning. In other (say mid-week) meetings it is more appropriate to deal with detailed arguments for creation against evolution, but our purpose in this lesson will be to allow the *Genesis* account to speak for itself.

Lesson Outline

Mention that people have always been curious about the origin of this world, the universe and themselves, but how can they discover their beginnings?

Who knows? One thing is certain, no scientist or historian was around when the universe was 'born'. No one saw the sun and moon when they first shone, and even the plants and animals were there before people arrived on the scene. So we have no eyewitness account of the beginning of the world. Outside God's Word, there is only guesswork and highly imaginative interpretations of the 'evidence'.

The Bible is unique in that it claims to be God's own account of how He made the world. The same God Who created the universe and everything in it, inspired the words of *Genesis 1*. What better authority could we have? Let us examine the account which goes right back to the very beginning of all things. Point out that atheistic scientists have tried to account for the beginning of this universe with ideas such as the 'big bang' theory, but they can only go so far back. Always their explanations beg the question, 'And where did *that* come from?'

In the beginning. By contrast with other schemes and theories, the Bible begins right at the beginning. It tells us that before anything began God was there. *In the beginning, God (Genesis 1.1* and *John 1.1)*. This is what we have to grasp first. Some people ask the question, 'And where did God come from?' The answer is that God did not come from anywhere; He was always there. He did not have a beginning because He was, and is, and always will be the ever-living God.

Explain to the children that so often when we think of God we imagine Him to be like us, having a beginning and end, living in time and space, and limited to a physical existence. Point out that God is altogether greater than us. He has no beginning or end. He is eternal. He lives above time and can look down upon us – like a helicopter pilot who sees the entire length of a road, while the person walking along it does not know what to expect as he rounds the next bend.

Nor is God confined to a physical frame like us. He is a

Spirit and can see all, and be everywhere at once. Though we cannot comprehend such a great Being, we must accept that He is far, far greater than we are. The Bible begins by telling us that it was this God Who made the entire universe.

Day 1 – Light. The Bible tells us elsewhere – *God is light, and in him is no darkness at all.* The first thing that God made, in keeping with His character, was light. God is good and pure and holy. He never needs to hide and work in the shadows – as sinful creatures do – and He sees everything as if in broad daylight. Thus, even before He made the sun, moon and stars, He made light and there was day and night on the very first day. At first He generated the light from Himself to teach us that the sun is merely His 'agent'. If necessary, He could dispense with it.

Day 2 – Skies. On the second day, God made the skies with the waters above and beneath them. 'But,' someone may say, 'I thought these things took millions of years, yet the Bible talks as if they took only seconds.' Once again we must remember that we are speaking of God Who made the great laws of nature which we observe and Who can also transcend them.

Measuring time. Give the class an illustration along these lines. Imagine a great modern city being built in a short space of time (eg: Canberra, Singapore or a Latin American city). Now let us suppose a country boy arriving in the city has never seen the modern machinery with which the city was built. One day the question dawns on his mind – how long did it take to build this city? A picture of the small, village builder digging foundations springs to his mind. He pictures many small vans and lorries being needed to gather in all the building materials. He wonders how long it took to erect such high blocks with only ladders and scaffolding to help. His conclusion? The city must have taken hundreds, if not thousands of years to build!

Of course, he is wrong. If only he had seen or read about huge modern cranes, giant pile-drivers, earth-movers and diggers, he would have realised that the city could be built in under ten years.

Explain to the class that we think rather like this boy. We

forget, or refuse to believe, that by His great power, in a mighty creative act, God was able to bring the world into being in a short space of time. Once He had finished this amazing work, He ordered everything to operate under the laws of nature that we see at work today. *Now* a tree needs many years of light, water and oxygen to grow, but *then* God's command was sufficient to bring it into being in a moment of time.

Today great earth tremors move mountains only a few inches, but *then* the seas and the dry land were completely separated the moment that God ordered that it should be done. Once we believe in God, it is easy to understand *that the worlds were prepared by the word of God (Hebrews 11.3).*

Laws come later. Today we measure time by a different set of principles from those in operation at the time of creation. To return to our city illustration, during the building of a city, earth-movers, tractors and cranes are free to move wherever they need, left or right, forwards and backwards, over grass verges and across open spaces. But once the city is built, strict laws are brought into operation. Traffic must keep to the left (or right!), move in lanes, stop at red traffic lights, obey signs, etc, or chaos and tragedy will ensue.

Similarly, laws of nature which are slow and gentle are now in operation for our benefit, though at the time of creation these were not in force. *Then*, God acted freely at great speed. *Now*, He has set His physical laws in operation. *Then*, He was able to achieve more in a day than we can now achieve in a thousand years.

Of course, God is still able to put His laws in abeyance and overrule them, as the Lord Jesus did when He performed His mighty miracles, but normally these great natural laws operate so that we are provided with an orderly world.

An almighty God. Our answer, therefore, to our young friend is: Yes, it would appear to us who judge the past by the present, that the universe took millions, if not billions of years to create. But once we understand the mighty power of God, then we grasp that He could easily overrule natural laws and do great things. It is a foolish person who sneers at the Bible because it records events which are supernatural. If we believe in God we should expect Him to do great things. The events of these six days are no exception.

Far-fetched? We may also like to suggest that the stretching of credulity comes rather from the evolutionist's position. If it were possible (and there is no sound evidence for this) for one animal to turn gradually into another, it would take hundreds of thousands of years. For the process to cover the immense variety of species seen today, even more millions of years must be invented – stretching the imagination far more than the account in *Genesis*.

Older classes will be interested to hear that even many secular scientists have admitted the impossibility of the theory of evolution, and these scientists are busy suggesting alternative explanations. How foolish not to accept the Creator's own account of the beginning of life. Yet such is the hostility of man towards God that any far-fetched alternative is preferred to the belief that God made us.

Application. Close this lesson by turning the class to *Isaiah 40*. Urge them to obey verse 26, to 'lift up their eyes' and learn the greatness of God. The glories of His creation leave man without excuse for unbelief *(Romans 1.20)*. Argue Isaiah's case (vv 17-18) that such a great God cannot be confined to human physical terms. He is not like us or anything we can make or conceive. No man-made theory can ever provide a viable alternative to belief in God. Yet He is willing to give strength and help to all who will earnestly seek Him (vv 28-31).

Best of all this great Lord God desires to *tend His flock* like a shepherd and *gather the lambs* in His arm. Ask the children if they knew that the mighty Maker and Sustainer of the whole universe desires to do so for them. Overwhelm them with this amazing picture of God's love and care. Help them to feel shame for their careless indifference and outright rebellion towards the Lord. Remind them of His willingness to receive and gather all those who return in repentance to this heavenly Shepherd.

Visual Aid

Teachers may find it helpful to make a scrapbook for the lessons on creation. Each day of creation can be illustrated in turn and related to the texts. Children could bring illustrations and suggestions of their own. This form of visual aid will not only act as a memory aid but provide a visual focal point for the lessons.

The Creation of Life and Man (7)

Genesis 1.9-31, and 2.1-25

Aim: To continue the narrative of God's creation. To emphasise the importance of His last and best creation, human beings, and to make the children aware of the sin of forsaking the Lord.

Teachers' Introduction

We continue last week's theme, taking up the creation account at day three. This week we shall want to emphasise the theme of *Psalm 8* – the honour with which God endowed man. Although we shall leave the subject of the Fall until next week, man's failure to live up to the Lord's high intentions for him will become glaringly obvious. As soon as the children are told what they were meant to be, it will be impossible for them not to notice the shortfall. This will provide the opportunity to present the Gospel with real relevance.

Lesson Outline

Day 3 – Dry land and life. On the third day, God divided the land from the sea and made the dry land. He dressed the earth with the covering of trees and grass and herbs. Emphasise these points:

(a) **Beauty and detail.** The amazing nature of the earth's covering with myriads of trees and flowers and plants, each one perfectly shaped; the enormous strength of the huge cedars, contrasted with the meticulous detail of the tiniest plant. The earth exhibits the marks of an artist as well as an architect. The world displays not only brilliant design but beauty and perfection. Photographers and painters are satisfied to make copies of these wonderful sights; scientists probe and discover the laws which keep them in motion, but God designed them all in the first place. The suggestion that these magnificent landscapes with their intricate hidden processes came about merely by chance seems more absurd the more we think about it.

(b) Ready for occupation. Remind older classes that when God made the world, He made it to look perfect and beautiful from the start. He did not plant it with seedlings but full-grown trees. The world and everything in it was created with an apparent vast age – adult trees, complete with many rings in their trunks, and so forth.

Day 4 – Sun, moon and stars. Next God made the sun, moon and stars to divide time into days and seasons.

(a) Perfect timing. Consider another fact we take for granted: the perfection and precision of the universe's time-clock. Describe how accurate tide timetables and lighting-up charts are. As long as man has lived, the world has never significantly slowed down, nor has it ever stopped on its multi-million-mile journey around the sun each year. Does this all happen by accident?

(b) Made to please. Even more amazing is the fact that the great cycles of nature coincide with the needs of the creatures living on earth, meeting both their need for food, clothing and fuel, and also their need of beauty and variety in the environment.

Day 5 – Living creatures. On the fifth day we are told that God began to make living creatures. First, He made those that live in the seas and rivers, from tiny minnows to great whales, as well as the birds of the air. Why do many of these have characteristics in common with one another? As we should expect, the one great Designer used the same features in many animals, birds and fish.

Evolution or creation? The fact that one fish resembles another confirms the fact that they have the same Maker. But the person who claims that this similarity proves that both developed from a common ancestor has an impossible problem to solve. How is it that while one fish has the same eyes as another, certain other characteristics may be totally different? Struggle as evolutionists might to produce a chart which shows a straightforward evolutionary development, they cannot truly achieve it. Endless pieces in the puzzle just do not fit.

Day 6 – Animals and people. On the sixth day, God created all the land animals, cattle, creeping things and beasts of the earth. Living in sheltered towns we seldom have the opportunity to see these creatures with their very diverse appearance and patterns of behaviour. Even on television or in the zoo we cannot fully appreciate all the skills and unique characteristics of different animals, insects, etc. But unprejudiced observation says, 'The hand that made them is divine.'

Even people who refuse to believe in God are forced to use personal terms when describing and accounting for the subtleties of any animal's design and behaviour. They say, 'Nature has given this animal these features.' *Nature* almost becomes a living creator! Have we noticed how the nature documentaries on television tend to credit animals with the power to change their features as they adapt to their needs and surroundings? Jesus reminded us that even a human being cannot *add one cubit unto his stature (Matthew 6.27, AV)* no matter how much thought he gives to it. Some biologists dismiss the notion of God, yet they credit the simplest creatures with God-like ability!

When God was satisfied that all His creation was *good*, He determined to create people, not just as a by-product, but as the zenith of His creation. The first man was quite different from the animals for he was made in God's own image. He was not a god, yet in some special ways he reflected God. Unlike the animals he had a *soul* breathed into him by the Lord. This means that the 'inner person' which is the real 'you' is immortal and capable (as originally made) of speaking to God, loving Him and obeying Him. How very different from the animals!

Along with the soul went two other things: the conscience and the reason. We have a knowledge of right and wrong, and we have the power to think. Teach the children about these three special gifts which belong only to human beings – the soul, the conscience and the reason.

We have only to compare a colony of apes with a modern city made by man to see how many 'missing links' are needed if the theory of evolution is ever to be established. Language, clothing, organisation, building, music, libraries, schools, places of worship, etc, are only some of the items missing from the animal kingdom and yet common to every part of the world where we find people. God made a garden for Adam the first man, and He also made from him a wife to be a worthy helper and companion.

Day 7 – Sabbath. At this point the creation was complete and perfect. God saw that all He had made was *very good*, and He rested from all His work, forever setting mankind the pattern of a day set apart.

What went wrong we shall discover next week. But this week we should remember that this account of the world's creation is the best. It tells us that there is a God Who made and designed it all and Who made us the highest of His creatures with special powers to know and love and obey Him. Do you respect and love your Maker? Did you realise that you owe your existence to the Lord God? Does God enjoy your fellowship or do you behave like a stranger? Do you exploit and enjoy His blessings without giving thought for Who provided them? Do you take for granted all the good things and blame God for all the bad things? The Bible urges, *Remember also your Creator in the days of your youth (Ecclesiastes 12.1).*

The Fall of Man (8)

Genesis 3

Aim: To show how great man's sin is. To explain the present fallen state of this world. To open up the Lord's way of forgiveness.

Teachers' Introduction

Great principles are to be tackled in this lesson. In a world which parades its high technology, but cannot explain human cruelty and weakness, young people are very receptive on hearing the Bible's unique explanation of man's contradictory nature. Here alone can mankind's lofty ideals *and* his woeful performance be accounted for. Here alone can the enigma of the human race be explained – wonderful gifts and abilities and tender emotions combined with extreme greed, selfishness and ruthlessness. Furthermore, this explanation can be given in such a way that the smallest 'Beginner' will understand, and the oldest member of the Bible Class respect, the doctrine of the Fall.

As the children return home it should be our desire that they will do so with real sorrow in their hearts, as they come to see the nature and extent of human sin towards God. They should see that the ugliness which surrounds them in this world is repugnant to God and has been entirely caused by the human race deliberately trampling on God's commands. And young people should be overwhelmed with wonder that God should still find it in His heart to love ungrateful, rebellious people, and to keep open the way of forgiveness and new life.

Lesson Outline

Describe the state of affairs that prevailed at the opening of this lesson. Each of the following points are featured in the suggested visual aid (VA 2) on pages 48-49.

(a) Man, higher than the animals, made in the *image of God* and imbued with a *living soul* was placed in a perfect world which God designated as 'very good'.

(b) He was given *dominion over all the creatures* upon earth (*Genesis 1.26*) and to him fell the privilege of naming the animals as they were presented to him by the Lord (*Genesis 2.19*).

(c) Even this kingdom did not satisfy the Lord as being good enough for man, and in addition to these blessings, and the Garden which God had specially planted, God made a perfect companion and helper for him. Eve, the first woman, who was part of his very self, became his wife (*Genesis 2.22-24*). Help the children to see that the first couple had everything that they could desire or dream.

(d) They knew the *companionship of the Lord*. They were in no way frustrated or bored having the whole universe to explore in company with its Designer. They had a breath-takingly beautiful landscape to tend, as well as the obedience and powers of the animals at their command. Adam and Eve, before they were tempted, were themselves perfect and upright. They were pure, they never lied and no shadow of deceitfulness crossed their minds. They did not know how to be selfish, angry or unkind. They could trust one another completely, and of course they loved the Lord their God. Without sin in their lives they knew no fear or guilt or suspicion, and not even the effects of the ageing process spoilt this paradise.

A greater gift. Even the fallen worldling values freedom highly, and God bestowed this great gift also on our first parents. Human beings were not to be slaves to God's wishes as fortunate but fettered creatures. Instead, God allowed them the great privilege of serving their Maker from grateful and willing hearts. This entailed the possibility and opportunity of their going another way. It meant that they could, if they wished, turn against the Lord and experiment with an 'alternative' way of living.

There was in the garden planted by the Lord a tree whose fruits opened up the possibility for man of knowing and experiencing an alternative 'scene' to one of perfection and holiness. This scene would come into existence only if Adam and Eve looked away from God. Explain to the youngest that Adam and Eve were not chained to God. Though warned of the terrible consequences, they were free to disobey. God did not remove from their reach the forbidden tree.

The Fall. Describe the events and their implications. The first sin was many sins combined together. It was not merely the taking of a fruit. Think of all the sins that led to the eating of the fruit.

(a) Charges against God. The serpent, used by Satan, began by suggesting that God was unfair to withhold a tree from their possession – and Eve was ready to believe it. How easily we believe anything which is said against God. How hard we find it to trust Him and His Word – even little children.

(b) God – a liar? Instead of turning away in disgust, Eve listened on as the devil called God a liar. God had said they would die – the devil said this was not true. At this point Eve should have been alarmed. She knew the Lord never lied, yet Eve was willing to doubt God's words of warning.

(c) Ingratitude and greed. The serpent persuaded her that God was keeping from her something exciting. He was being unfair to her. He was keeping her down by not permitting this fruit. If she ate the fruit (said the serpent), she would be as great as God, able to know about all kinds of things which were being withheld from her. She was ungrateful and unappreciative of her incredible blessings, and lusted after this 'secret world'. Today the human race still shows no appreciation to God for life's benefits, and everyone lusts to have more. Eve wanted more, but her rebellion was not only to end in disaster for her, but also for those for whom she was responsible as *the mother of all the living (Genesis 3.20).*

(d) Pride, disobedience, stealing. How proud Eve became in that moment as she thought she knew better than God and could disregard His warnings. How proud she was to think she could cope with a world full of evil as well as good. She was also disobedient, because she went full against what God had plainly said. She became a rebel. And she also became a thief, for she took what did not belong to her. Are not these our sins too? We think very highly of ourselves. We take no notice of God's commandments, and we steal our lives for ourselves.

(e) Excuses. Help the class to see that Eve tried to soothe her conscience by pretending that her decision hinged on the mere matter of taking pleasant fruit which could only do her good. Deep in her heart she must have known that she was despising the gifts of God, dismissing His friendship, accusing Him of lying and using the influence He had given her to persuade her husband to go along with her in this act of treachery. But she claimed it was a simple act of taking some good-looking fruit. This was the sin of self-justification. How often have we done the same? How often do we persuade ourselves that lies and other sins are excusable?

The results. Far from refusing Eve's suggestion and rebuking her, Adam also agreed to eat the forbidden fruit. He should have known better but instead he went along with her suggestion and joined in her sins. The first effect of this act was one of shame. For the first time Adam and Eve experienced shame and insecurity. Suddenly they wanted to

Fit for HEAVEN
↑
FREEDOM
↑
The friendship of the LORD GOD
↑
Eve especially made for Adam
↑
Dominion over the animals & plants
↑
The Garden of Eden
↑
A living soul
↑
Were GIVEN
↑
Made in the image of God

- -

ADAM and EVE

Believed Satan rather than God
↓
Became
↓
Ungrateful
↓
Greedy
↓
Proud
↓
Disobedient
↓
Rebellious
↓
Thieves
↓
and then covered sin with excuses
↓
fit for HELL

See instructions   on opposite page...

VA 2 – *Visual Aid for use with Lesson 8 – 'The Fall of Man'*

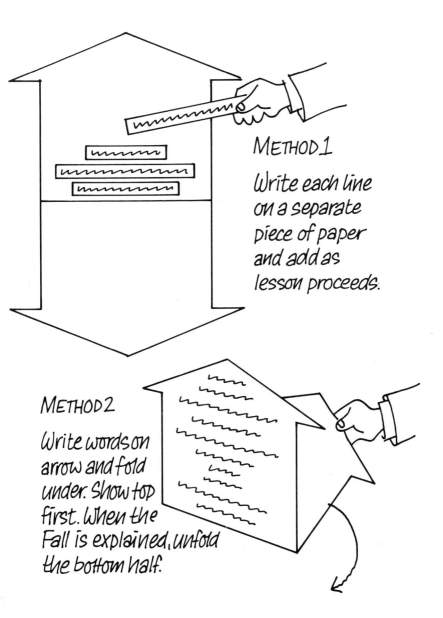

METHOD 1

Write each line on a separate piece of paper and add as lesson proceeds.

METHOD 2

Write words on arrow and fold under. Show top first. When the Fall is explained, unfold the bottom half.

cover and hide themselves. They knew that despite their attempt to justify the deed (v 6), they had behaved very ungratefully, proudly, selfishly and despicably. For the first time it was necessary for them to run away from God. Soon they were lying to cover their sin. They had become dishonest hypocrites.

The fact that they ran away from God condemned them, as it does so many others. Why do so many children stay away from God's house – and adults too? Is there anything wrong in God? Or is the evil in us? God knew at once why Adam and Eve were behaving so strangely and He summoned them to Him to announce the awful consequences of their sin:–

(a) The entry of spiritual death – human beings would now be cut off from knowing God as Guide and Friend.

(b) The entry of physical death into the world.

(c) The entry of sorrow and labour into the world, for men, women and the whole creation.

(d) The forfeiture of eternal life in the presence of God.

(e) The exile of the human race from the Garden of Eden.

Explain to the children that this important chapter in *Genesis* is no fairy-tale. It is the only credible explanation for our world as we know it. This is how the highest being in God's creation – with a soul, a conscience and the power of reason – became a weak, fallen being, cut off from God. If we understand this chapter, we shall understand what we read in the newspapers and see on television. We shall be wiser than many psychologists and politicians – even though we are only children *(Psalm 119.99)* – and we shall understand ourselves.

We shall know that men and women were made by God to know and love Him, and this is why we have moral standards in our hearts – a knowledge of right and wrong – which no animal has. But because our first parents deliberately chose another way, we are 'fallen' beings, and we cannot live up to these standards. Sometimes we have the longing to be clean and right yet we are powerless to achieve this. Even governments talk of freedom, justice and rights when all the time they are full of violence, corruption and sin. Only the Bible explains this 'contradiction' in the human race.

God's lovingkindness. What did God do about the Fall of

the human race? He promised a Saviour. Because we are incapable of reforming ourselves He promised a Deliverer, One Who would take the punishment of our sin for us, and conquer Satan. The class should know His name. Urge them to see how sin has wound itself around them. Remind them that they are powerless to overcome it. Speak to them of the Lord Jesus Who alone can rescue them, and show them that by turning to Him, they will be doing the exact opposite of Eve. And as they receive the Lord's forgiveness He will restore them to the place which Adam lost – only it will be even better. They will know the friendship of the Lord day by day and look forward to living with Him for ever in Heaven. As Isaac Watts put it,

> *Where He displays His healing power,*
> *Death and the curse are known no more;*
> *In Him the tribes of Adam boast*
> *More blessings than their father lost.*

Cain and Abel (9)
Living Away From God

Genesis 4.1-16

Aim: To show that if we stubbornly persist in ignoring the Lord's gracious reasoning with us, we shall live to reap the bitter consequences.

Teachers' Introduction.

This lesson rings so true to life as we know it. By drawing this caricature of men and women in their state of foolish unreasonableness, we must try to show the children a wiser path. With younger classes, avoid dwelling on the aspect of sacrifice in Abel's offering, better to concentrate on the lesson of coming to the Lord with the right attitude.

Lesson Outline

Ask the class to consider what it is like to leave home. At first the suggestion might seem attractive. They would be free to stay up as long as they liked! There would be no parents to tell them off or complain. But soon they would miss a warm home, meals prepared, clothes washed and above all, the love of a family unit. They would find themselves weighed down by pressures and responsibilities unknown before.

Remind the class of last week's lesson, when Adam and Eve proudly rebelled against the Lord and chose to do without Him. Outside the Garden of Eden they had to toil and labour. Instead of the birth of children being a delight, it was to involve pain and sorrow. Worst of all, they could not enjoy the close friendship of the Lord as they had done in Eden. Yet we are going to see how one member of the family stubbornly held out in this state of enmity and rebellion, and reaped the bitter consequences. Let us see what happened to Eve's two sons, so that we can learn from them.

Two kinds of gift. Cain and Abel both had to work for a living. Abel kept the flocks and Cain cultivated crops. Although they had fallen from God's blessing, yet they both acknowledged God and brought an offering to the Lord. One gift pleased the Lord, the other did not. At first this seems very strange, but we shall soon see the reason why. And when we find the answer to this mystery it will show us whether or not we are in the same danger as Cain.

Cain's gift. Cain's gift was rejected by God because it was given in the wrong spirit. God did not *need* Cain's offering. He owns the universe, so what need would He have for a bundle of corn? Yet God graciously receives the smallest gift if it comes as a token of trust, gratitude and love. But Cain's gift signified none of these. How do we know? Because when the Lord showed no regard for it, Cain grew angry and sullen.

Cain's offering was proud. He was showing off his produce and his farming expertise. He was claiming to be successful and capable, and he expected God to accept him because of what he had accomplished. (Teachers of classes with younger children can give an example of how present-day children might do this.) Cain only presented an offering to God so that he would get some reward. When this was rejected he was enraged.

Ask the class if they ever think like this. Do they imagine that their lives are likely to be approved by God? Millions of adults think like this. When they hear the Christian message telling them that they need complete forgiveness before God can receive them, they become very angry and offended. They begin to protest, saying that they do many good things. But the tiny bit of 'good' which people may do cannot make up for all the bad.

An explanation. Even so, God graciously came to Cain and reasoned with him. Tell the children that it is essential to listen when we are corrected. If we assemble a part on our bicycle or car back to front, it would be a favour for a friend to tell us so, and to warn of the consequences of leaving it uncorrected. Let the children see how absurd it would be to stamp our feet and refuse to listen. Stubborn pride will only make us look ridiculous in the end.

Anger follows pride. Yet when the Lord told Cain of his error, and the possibility of correcting it, he would not listen. His pride was hurt and the outcome was hatred and jealousy towards his brother. Do we resent God's Word to us? Do we hate to hear that we are sinful? Does the Gospel annoy us? Tell the class that many Christians have had to bury their pride and admit that their idea of pleasing God had been all wrong, and humbly accept God's own way of salvation. Martin Luther is an obvious example. He had to learn that doing his best was not good enough to fit him for Heaven. Have we ever learned this lesson? Tell how he was once a monk, and how he thought that whipping and cutting his body to make himself humble would be rewarded by God. But he came to realise all this was of no use; he must trust God alone to save him.

A warning. The Lord warned Cain that if he stubbornly refused to learn from his mistake, he stood in great danger. He must approach God in the same spirit that Abel had. When he approached God he must humbly ask forgiveness of his sins. Then he must yield his life to God and follow His guidance. He must draw all his help from God. If he would not do this, then, said the Lord, sin would be always at the door of his life (v 7). It would shadow him, and wait for him every morning. The only way for Cain to get to Heaven would be to defeat sin by his own efforts – and that, of course, would be impossible. In other words, God warned

Cain that if a person will not ask for forgiveness, and seek conversion, then that person will be 'on his own' in the battle of life, and go to hell at the end of life's journey.

Excuses. After his rejection, jealousy simmered in Cain's heart, and his brother became the object of blame. The children will be familiar with this kind of situation. How often a boy dropped from the school football team finds fault with the player who has replaced him! How quickly children grow bitter towards those who seem to gain greater approval!

Explain that this can happen with us when the Gospel points out our sin to us. Instead of receiving His word and repenting, we begin to make excuses. Often we blame God Himself for our failings. Sometimes we blame Christians. Secretly we envy their trust in the Lord, their changed way of life, but instead of following them, we resent them, and the Lord they love.

Murder. Cain and Abel met in a field. We do not know what was said, but it is probable that Abel's godly conversation pricked Cain's conscience and inflamed his jealousy. Quickly his hatred rose to such a pitch that he killed his own brother. Now, even Cain must have realised that his sin was very great, though he still complained at his punishment saying that it would be 'too hard to bear'. Show how he had to be sent away from his family and from the Lord to live a life of fear and toil. Help the children to feel the tragedy of this situation, especially as it was so unnecessary. Urge them not to allow foolish pride to keep them away from the Saviour.

A better way. Describe Abel's offering. It was not an offering which Abel had thought of by himself – a good way of showing off and displaying his achievements. We believe that Abel was doing what God had previously asked people to do. He was offering a sacrifice. A sacrifice was a picture intended to show that someone must suffer and die in our place, to take away our sin. All the sacrifices of old taught the people that one day a Saviour would come to pay the price, so making forgiveness possible. When God said that a sacrifice was to be made in worship He was teaching men and women that before they come to worship Him, they must understand how serious their sin is.

It is not right to skip into the Lord's presence and to pray with a few easy words. We have to understand that our sin has made us worthy of eternal death, and that if we are to be saved, someone must die. The wonderful message of the Bible is that God has sent His own Son, the Lamb of God, to die for the sins of all those who will believe in Him and place their trust in all that He did for them at Calvary. No wonder that Isaac Watts voiced the words:

> *When I survey the wondrous cross,*
> *On which the Prince of Glory died,*
> *My richest gain I count but loss,*
> *And pour contempt on all my pride.*

Plead with your class not to join the masses of people who will go down to hell because of foolish pride. Encourage them to think of the perfect Prince of Glory Who, though He had never sinned, was willing to suffer deep humiliation on the cross, in order to rescue worthless sinners.

Noah (10)

Genesis 6.5 – 9.17; Matthew 24.37-42

Aim: To show how sin grieves the Lord. To compare the days of Noah with our own, as the Saviour did, and to sound a serious note of warning. To demonstrate God's mercy in finding a way of escape in every generation for those who believe Him.

Teachers' Introduction

And the Lord was sorry that He had made man on the earth, and He was grieved in His heart. These must be some of the most tragic words ever written. For a moment the Holy Spirit draws aside the veil and shows how our sin affects the heart of almighty God. Adults may harden themselves to these words or hurry on to the next verse, but children with young and tender hearts will be touched at such a description (*Genesis 6.5-7*). In our constant effort to show that sin is much more than certain misdeeds and actions, that it includes our whole attitude to our Maker, these verses will be invaluable. We must not give the impression that having made the world and man, God suddenly changed His mind.

These words are not intended to describe God's character literally, for He never changes. He is 'without bodily parts and passions'. These words show us, in language we can understand, that our sin is so great and grievous that it affects the very heart of God. If children can grasp this, then by God's grace they will appreciate the love of the Saviour in giving His life for sinners. This lesson is one of those Old Testament Gospel gems which should excite every teacher.

Lesson Outline

Encourage the children to remember an occasion of bitter disappointment. They may have painstakingly made an item which they had to discard in the end. Some may have spent time and trouble beating a cake mixture only to consign it to the bin because it turned out flat and stodgy. Others may have devoted hours of labour and thought to renovating a toy or bicycle only to discover that it had a major weakness and would have to be discarded after all. Describe the heart-break of a farmer who has to destroy his herd of cattle, the work of a lifetime, when they are found to have foot-and-mouth disease.

Tell the class how great God is, that He knows the beginning from the end, that He never changes His mind, and that even before Adam had sinned, He had made plans to send the Saviour. Yet at the same time God is so great that the Bible discloses that He feels more sorrow for our sin and its consequences than we feel ourselves.

God's sorrow. The first part of our lesson tells us that when God looked at the earth He had made, back in the days of Noah, He was sorry that He had made man, because man's wickedness was so great. It was not that men and women *occasionally* failed and disobeyed, but *every imagination of the thoughts of his heart was only evil CONTINUALLY (Genesis 6.5, AV)*. We might imagine that looking down from Heaven, God would write mankind off, as a businessman writes off a bad loss. Instead the Bible tells us that it grieved God in His heart (v 6).

Next ask the class how they imagine they stand in God's eyes. When He looks at their lives, is He pleased? Does He see individuals who love Him, speak to Him, and are never so happy as when they are serving and obeying Him as their

heavenly Father? Or does He see young people who want
nothing to do with Him, who think only of themselves and
find pleasure and enjoyment in breaking His commands and
insulting His name? Help the children to feel what this
means to the Lord Who made them and who loves them.
Show them that while they carelessly sin and light-heartedly
misuse His name, God's heart is grieved and full of sorrow.
Perhaps they have never considered this.

The consequences. As a result of man's sin, God chose to
destroy an evil generation from the face of the earth. He
decided to send a great flood from which no living creature
could escape.

The Bible tells us elsewhere that God will one day judge
our world at the end of time, not with water, but with fire
(2 Peter 3.10). People behave like a criminal who presumes
all policemen are fools, and is confident that he will never be
caught. People imagine that God cannot see and will not do
anything about their rebellion. But be warned!

Kindness. Describe the genuineness of God's sorrow.
Having decided to destroy mankind, God was still ready to
show His mercy to Noah and his family. It was not that Noah
was without sin or perfect, but unlike his fellow men, Noah
was anxious to obey God, and instead of ignoring Him, he
walked with God (v 9). For the sake of this one man, God was
willing to delay His judgement and to make elaborate plans
for his safety.

Explain that God is still the same. He delayed judgement
on Sodom for the sake of Lot. He is postponing the final day
of judgement so that He can safely gather in those boys, girls
and adults who believe in Him and desire to please Him.

The ark. No doubt the class will be confident that they
know all about Noah's ark, so ask them for some facts and
figures! Ask them for its size; how many decks did it have,
from what was it made? Teachers who do not know all
the answers and who find translating cubits into modern
measurements an ordeal, will find the answers presented in a
very vivid way in *The Genesis Flood* by Morris and Whit-
comb, page 10. The writers conclude: 'The ark was about
13,960 tons, which should place it well within the category of

large metal ocean-going vessels today.' Describe how the Lord instructed Noah to build this great boat which would house him, his family and a pair of all the living creatures during the Flood*.

Explain how silly Noah must have looked to his unbelieving contemporaries. He believed and obeyed God despite their scorn and derision, and we must do the same. Worldlings still scoff at those who believe the Lord and take His commands seriously, and the Lord Jesus warned that we must expect this if we follow Him.

Too late. Suggest that Noah was under more pressure than we are. After all, he was building a huge boat in the middle of a field, nowhere near to a deep river or sea. This must have seemed outrageously funny to those who wanted an excuse to poke fun at this man who believed God. But before long they were not laughing. As the waters poured down from above and erupted from beneath, they screamed out with fear and terror. The very thing which Noah had warned them about was happening and it was too late for them to repent. Only Noah's family were safe, the Lord Himself having shut them safely within the ark. No matter how much it rained, they were secure.

Noah's society – our society. Use the words of the Saviour to show how similar our society is to that of Noah's. The end of the world moves nearer, but mankind goes on organising his affairs without taking into consideration any possibility of an end. Individuals busy themselves with eating, drinking and enjoyment, without making any serious provision for death – which is the only really certain event in life! Help the class to see the situation objectively and to acknowledge how silly we are. Remind them of the weeping and wailing which the Lord Jesus predicted, when the day of judgement catches people unawares. Urge your children not to be caught out.

An escape. Describe how the Lord has designed a

*Dimensions of the ark: length 450 ft; width 25 ft; height 45 ft. Internal capacity equal to over 500 large railway freight-wagons. Three floors (or decks) averaging 15 ft headroom. Barge-like in shape; no space wasted on engine rooms or fuel tanks (the ark was not going anywhere!).

wonderful way of rescuing us. Those who believe the Lord and who experience conversion, will find a way of escape on the day of judgement. They will shelter, not in an ark, but in the arms of the Lord Himself *(Matthew 23.37)*. He faced the fury of God's righteous anger on our behalf at the cross of Calvary. Urge your class to wake up, to leave the mindless, scoffing crowds who dismiss God's urgent warnings, and to seek the shelter provided by the Lord for all who are truly sorry for their past attitude and sins, and who want to please Him from now on.

Revision (11)
Revision of lesson series 1 and 2
– Mark (part 1) and Genesis (part 1)

Lessons 1 – 10

Aim: To convince children, surrounded by an atheistic society, that they have a Creator and that they should remember Him while they are still young *(Ecclesiastes 12.1)*.

Teachers' Introduction

A revision lesson should never be treated with less enthusiasm than other lessons. It has several functions:–

(a) To help the children remember lessons in the context of the whole series and to impress upon them the overall theme. We can draw these two particular series of lessons fittingly together by reminding the children that the Lord Jesus, when He came to live on earth, demonstrated by His mighty power that He was God and that He was present at the creation of the world.

(b) The art of teaching is said to be repetition. If children are told something once they *may* remember it, but they are much more likely to remember it if they are taught it twice. The time-honoured system of revision and examination has proved itself down the years, and although we are not solemnly examining children, we can take advantage of this technique to fix our message in their memories.

(c) Revision lessons, while appearing to test the pupil, in fact examine the teacher! This lesson gives us an opportunity to assess our term's work and to adjust our approach accordingly for the coming term. When we discover that certain concepts are confused in the children's minds, we shall be stirred to adjust our approach. Should we simplify our presentation, or illustrate more? Do we need to be more animated and lively?

(d) The revision lesson can also be an opportunity for the children to question us and raise their difficulties. We may be surprised to discover children asking such basic questions as, 'But why does God punish sin? How can someone know they are a Christian? How exactly do you repent?' If children are anxious to ask such questions it will be better to abandon a questionnaire and let them freely air their problems.

The revision lesson needs to be prepared as carefully as any other lesson if it is to be fully useful. Younger and more lively classes may need a visual framework, and some form of reward for good answers would not be out of place. In particular, teachers need to think of questions which give an indication of their children's spiritual response. We should be especially watchful for any marks of grace. In an atheistic society such as ours, just a flicker of understanding may indicate the Lord working in a child's heart, and we should never despise or overlook such evidence.

Lesson Outline

The form of the lesson will vary with the age of the class. Examples of two kinds of approaches which could be used are given here:–

(1) An acrostic on the theme of the *Genesis* lessons which emphasises the theme common to both series for younger classes:–

C – the fifth word of the Bible is --- *(Genesis 1.1)*.

R – on the seventh day God --- *(Genesis 2.2)*.

E – God placed the first man and woman in the Garden of --- *(Genesis 2.8)*.

A – The name of the first man was --- *(Genesis 2.20)*.

T – When Eve saw that the tree was good for food and desirable to make one wise, she --- the fruit *(Genesis 3.6)*.

O – Adam and Eve stayed in the Garden until they sinned, then the Lord sent them --- *(Genesis 3.23)*.

R – After the great flood, God promised never to destroy the earth in this way again. The sign He gave to mankind was a --- (*Genesis 9.13*).

Children could also be asked to find the place of the missing word in their Bibles.

(2) The second part of the lesson could contain a more spiritually applied aspect relating to the *Jesus' Power* series. Using the visual-aid pentagon, ask questions such as the following:–

(a) What did Jesus do which showed His power over *nature*? Who can we trust to guide and protect us across the voyage of life? What question did the disciples ask about the Lord Jesus after they had seen this amazing miracle?

(b) How did Jesus demonstrate His power over *death*? What attitude did Jairus show when he came to Jesus? How should we approach the Lord? What kind of life is the Lord Jesus willing to give to us?

(c) Jesus showed His power over the *devil* by transforming a most helpless and hopeless case. Where did this demon-possessed man live? How do we know that Jesus went especially to save him? What did the Lord ask him to do after he had been made well? What should all Christians do for the Lord after He has saved them?

(d) How many people watched as Jesus displayed His great power over *need* and hunger? What did He use to feed this great crowd? Who gave Him this small meal? Jesus called Himself 'the Bread of Life' – what does this mean for us?

(e) On many occasions Jesus showed His power to heal all kinds of *illnesses*, at a word. Who did we learn about in particular? What was his problem? What can we learn from this man? In what sense are we blind? Who can open our eyes, so that we see and believe in the Saviour for ourselves?

Application. Close the lesson by reminding the class that all these lessons urge them to believe and trust the Lord Jesus Who proved His mighty power over all the great forces which threaten us. He was indeed the Son of God, Who made the whole universe. He will one day be our Judge. But He invites us here and now to seek Him as our Saviour.

Series 3
Mark's Gospel (Part II)
OPPOSITION TO JESUS

12 – Prejudice

Opposition to Jesus often begins with nothing more than hard-hearted stubbornness towards the Lord and His message, as demonstrated by the scribes in this lesson. Are our children entering on a collision course with their Maker because they will not consider His gracious call?

13 – Superiority and Pride

Having refused to respect the Saviour's claims, the Pharisees went on to justify themselves. They considered themselves righteous enough – indeed it was part of their so-called righteousness to disdain 'sinners'. Will pride and self-righteousness blind our children from seeing their need for a Saviour?

14 – Hardness and Hate

No one can remain neutral to the Saviour for long. Soon the scribes and Pharisees were plotting against Jesus and planning His death. Highly 'religious' people have often been His most bitter enemies. If young people do not love Him and follow Him they too will become hardened against Him.

15 – Hypocrisy

Jesus was often at pains to expose the hypocrisy and evil of the religious leaders of His day and to warn people about them. We must do the same.

16 – Dishonesty

When Jesus arrived in Jerusalem and saw the religious leaders, they were exposed as nothing more than a band of crooks, and He threw them out of the Temple. Soon they were guilty of demanding the death of God's Messiah without any lawful justification. Their satisfaction was great as they jeered at the dying Christ, but even then He was willing and able to forgive hardened scribes and Pharisees.

17 – How Can We Go to Heaven?

If many great religious leaders are bound for hell, who can be saved? Salvation depends not on us and our imagined goodness, but on God's mercy and love. This lesson examines the way which He made for sinners to return to Him.

Visual Aid

VA 3 (see pages 64-65) is designed for use throughout this series.

Prejudice (12)
The Paralytic Healed

Mark 2.1-12

Aim: To warn the children of the dangers of opposing the Saviour by refusing to change their minds, like the scribes.

Teachers' Introduction

This lesson is interesting in so many respects. Children have always been fascinated to hear of the determined efforts of these men to bring their friend to Jesus by such an unusual method of entry. Here at the beginning of the Saviour's ministry we see Him making His divine claims and performing a remarkable miracle to prove that He is the Son of God. Then we see Him exposing the prejudice and stubborn opposition of the scribes. This will give teachers the opportunity to show how many blessings have been missed because of *pride and stubborn prejudice.*

This visual aid comprises a large figure of a Pharisee, and two-sided cards to hang around his neck with thread. You may copy this figure, larger in size and mount on stiff card.

Print out five cards with the wording given opposite, with the correct words on the reverse of each card as shown.

Each week produce your Pharisee. As you recount the events, place card (side 1) over his shoulders. Then, as the Lesson is applied, reverse the card to show words on other side.

"My mind is made up—Jesus is not God's Son"

VA 3 – Visual Aid for use with 'Opposition to Jesus' lessons.

SIDE 1   SIDE 2

	Side 1		Side 2
1	"My mind is made up – Jesus is not God's Son"		PREJUDICED – Determined not to believe
2	"I would never eat with sinners"		PROUD – Too good to need a Saviour
3	"I must make Jesus look silly in public today"		HATEFUL – Looking for faults in God
4	"God must be so pleased with me – I keep all the Jewish rules"		HYPOCRITICAL – Pretending to be good
5	"Buy your sacrifices from me"		DISHONEST Using religion when there's something in it for me

Lesson Outline

Introduction. Remind the class that there were two responses to the Lord. Many people (especially among the Jews) saw His miracles and heard His teaching but did not believe in Him. Others followed Him and experienced a complete transformation of their lives. It is the same today. Around the world there are millions who have found Jesus to be their Lord and Saviour. But there are many more who refuse to recognise and believe Him.

How can this be? Why do the majority of people turn away from the one Person Who could turn their 'hell to Heaven'? They will queue and clamour to see some earthly hero. Why do they dismiss the King of kings and Lord of lords? Is it possible that some of our class could be among those who reject the Saviour?

Jesus back in Capernaum. Describe how crowds of people gathered when they heard that Jesus had arrived back in Capernaum. Why? Remind the class that they had heard about the amazing miracles which Jesus had done. Many wanted to be healed, and all were curious to hear the things which He was teaching. He did not bore them with long, dreary sermons, but He spoke clearly about the way to Heaven. They had never heard anything like it before.

Amongst the crowd that gathered were the 'clergy' of the day – the scribes and Pharisees. They were people who boasted that they were very religious. They wore religious clothes and were proud of their outwardly strict manner of life. We might have expected these men to be the first to welcome the Saviour, but instead they were very cynical.

Looking for trouble! They did not want God to intervene in their lives! They ran the 'church' of their country and they did not want a Messiah to take over! But chiefly they were wounded by the things which Jesus said about sin. He put His finger on *their* behaviour and sinful attitudes. Because they resented Jesus so much, they were filled with blind prejudice which made them quite unable to appreciate His great miracles. They just did not believe that these were performed by His divine power – even though they could not explain the amazing results.

Some of these men had come all the way from Jerusalem to try to find fault with the miracles of Jesus. They did not wish to be connected with His admirers and sat at the side like 'inspectors'. Do we approach the Saviour with the same critical attitude – the attitude which says, 'I'm interested in coming to Sunday School, but don't expect me to become religious'? (Older classes can be told about unbelieving liberal academics who sit in judgement over the Bible and its contents.)

Determination. Relate the unusual course of events so that the children are thoroughly intrigued. Help them to admire the determination of the four men who were not to be put off by the seeming impossibility of bringing their paralysed friend to Jesus. Help them to respect their initiative in making an opening in the roof.

Help the children to imagine the scene as a large hole appeared in the roof and the paralysed man was let down directly at the feet of Jesus. Suggest that if we were half as anxious to seek the Lord as these men, we would quickly find Him. Encourage young believers to have the same determination in bringing their friends to Jesus.

Forgiveness proved. Continue the narrative by explaining that just as everyone was expecting Jesus to heal the man, the Saviour turned to him and said, *My son, your sins are forgiven.* This had two dramatic effects. It *surprised* the people, but it *shocked* the scribes and Pharisees. They were outraged to hear the Saviour speaking like God by telling this man his sins were forgiven, and they instantly wanted to accuse Jesus of blasphemy.

Although they were too cowardly to state their accusation publicly, Jesus knew what they were thinking. (Jesus always knows what we are thinking.) Instead of denying the charge, He immediately took action to prove that He possessed the power of God. He commanded the paralysed man to rise from his bed and walk.

Describe the reaction of the man, his friends and the crowd. *They were all amazed and were glorifying God,* saying they had never seen anything like this before. Describe how glad the healed man must have felt. It was wonderful to be free to walk on earth, but even more, to be certain that he would one day walk the streets of Heaven. Ask the class for their list of priorities. Are they more concerned about their earthly and physical state than the well-being of their souls? Which did Jesus consider mattered most – even in the case of a severely handicapped person? What did He do first – heal the body or the soul?

The scribes and Pharisees. Were the scribes convinced by these amazing events? Did they come to realise that Jesus was their Messiah, sent from Heaven? No, they did not. Their minds were shut tight, and no amount of miracles would change them. Instead of gaining in respect for the Lord we see them condemning Him in a matter of days (*Mark 2.16*). They were not prepared to bow the knee to His rule and so they began to oppose Him.

If they had been *truly* religious, as they pretended to be, they would have rejoiced to see this miracle and would have recognised Jesus as their Lord and God. Instead, despite the joy and excitement of the occasion, we see them sitting sullen and unaffected. It was as though they heartily wished the man's healing had been a failure!

Before we condemn the scribes and Pharisees too much, is it possible that we are like them? When we hear God's Word do we receive it gladly? Or do we just resent it? If following Jesus means admitting our sins and changing our whole outlook on life, will we be as reluctant as the scribes?

Could we be wrong? Thousands of people will go to hell simply because of their prejudice. Before they even read the Bible or attend a Gospel church they have already made up their minds about God – that He does not exist or that He cannot be known. They stubbornly refuse to consider any other possibility. Some even refuse to enter a church. They are like people who have made up their minds that the earth is flat! Is it possible that someone in the class has been living with this attitude – perhaps unaware of how foolish it is? Like an ostrich burying its head in the sand, someone has possibly decided that there is no life after death, no God in Heaven, and no day of judgement. But what if that person is wrong?

The consequences of this attitude are terrible as we shall be learning. Before many years had gone by these very scribes and Pharisees were nailing God's Son to the cross, and were guilty of the greatest sin. Sin will never stop at prejudice and stubbornness. We must turn to the Saviour and ask Him to save us before these things rule us completely.

How greatly blessed those scribes could have been! They could have known the friendship and companionship of the Lord of Glory. Instead they cast away the opportunity in their prejudice.

Urge the children to take advantage of the great opportunity to follow Jesus, avoiding the mistakes of those scribes at all costs.

Superiority and Pride (13)
Jesus Calls Matthew and His Friends

Mark 2.13-17

Aim: To show the children how much they need to be forgiven by the Saviour, even though pride may tell them otherwise.

Lesson Outline

Introduction. Describe how crowds of people followed Jesus to the seaside to hear Him teach them about God and the importance of finding Him. Many people went to hear, including some who had no time for religion because they were more interested in making money and enjoying the things which it could buy. Nevertheless, even these wanted to hear Jesus because His preaching was different. Matthew was probably like this.

The cost. As Matthew listened to Jesus, he began to see how unstable and fleeting his ill-gotten gain was. Just as he had to prepare accounts for his Roman masters, so one day he began to realise that he would have to offer an account of his life to God, His Maker. He began to feel a great urge to put the matter right, but recoiled when he considered the cost.

Repentance for him would involve a completely new start to life and a break from everything he had previously enjoyed and lived for. He did not attempt to hide his sin or pretend it was not there, but to part company with it would not be easy. Remind the class that following the Lord still involves leaving behind the old life and making a total break with sin.

Follow Me! Go on to tell what happened when Jesus came to Matthew's place of work. Matthew had not found the strength or determination to make the necessary break with his sinful life, but when Jesus came to fetch him, he was ready to obey the Saviour's command. In that moment he saw vividly how hollow and vain his life had been. He grasped the opportunity of being called and accepted by the only Person Who was able to deal with all his despicable ways. Explain that Matthew's conversion meant the joy of knowing his sins were forgiven, the wonder of speaking to God's own Son, and the discovery of the value of spiritual blessings (or treasures) compared with earthly money.

Speak of his desire to share this great experience with his friends and colleagues, and his invitation for them to meet the Lord at his home. Explain that this desire to tell friends and family about the Saviour is common to all newly-converted Christians.

At Matthew's home. Re-create the atmosphere which you might imagine to have prevailed at this gathering. The worldly group was curious to meet Matthew's new Friend. They were surprised that Jesus was willing to dine with them, instead of disowning them and keeping His distance, as the other religious leaders did. They wanted to discover for themselves what there was about Christ that made Matthew willing to desert his lucrative profession to follow Him. Though they detested the normal religious teachers of their day, they were willing to give a hearing to someone who could really tell them about God.

Then show how something happened which could have ruined any chance of Matthew's friends hearing the message which they so badly needed. Just as the Lord Jesus had aroused the interest of these hardened men, the atmosphere was soured by the intrusion of a party of scribes and Pharisees. These had not been touched or moved by the wonderful miracles Jesus had done. They stubbornly refused to listen to His teaching no matter how wonderfully His power was demonstrated and proved. Instead they were determined to find fault. They discovered almost with glee that Jesus was breaking one of their self-imposed rules. He was eating with tax-gatherers! Describe their state of hypocritical shock and horror. Never for one moment would they have closely related themselves to such a person as Matthew.

To them it seemed an ideal moment to 'expose' Jesus, so they said to His disciples, *'Why is He eating and drinking with tax-gatherers and sinners?'* The Pharisees were insinuating that Jesus was unholy and defiled by mixing with sinful people. They believed that by mixing with sinners one was bound to become contaminated by them. The fact that Jesus mixed with such irreligious people was, in their view, proof enough that He could not possibly have come from God.

An illustration with four lessons. Jesus had heard their comments, and in a few simple sentences He was able to make the whole matter clear. Help the class to respect His method. Jesus used just one simple illustration which silenced the Pharisees and put the point beyond dispute.

(a) Ask the class – Who needs a doctor? People brimming with health are not to be found in the doctor's surgery. Who did Jesus come to save? Was it perfect people, or those whose lives were sick with sin? Jesus came as a *Saviour,* and therefore we expect to see Him dealing with the lost and needy souls He came to save.

(b) Doctors visit the sick yet they do not pick up all the illnesses themselves! (Who ever heard of someone who did not want to be a doctor for fear of getting all the diseases!) Of course God's Son was not contaminated by sinners because He spoke with them, any more than the doctor catches the diseases.

(c) Some people suffer and die because they will not see a doctor. They try to hide the symptoms, pretending that they do not exist. They do not want to face up to their illness, or the need to have an operation. The Pharisees were sinners too – being guilty of very many ugly sins – but they thought they had no need of a Saviour, and that they could put any 'little' problems right in their own way. What a foolish and proud mistake!

(d) The Saviour portrays Himself as a skilled and sincerely

interested doctor. He does not flatter and assure us all is well when it is not. He exposes our sin and finds a means to remove it. However painful the process of conversion, the result is the joy of forgiveness and recovery, as Matthew discovered. Have you ever faced up to your problem and searched for the Saviour? How tragic to miss the opportunity of a cure from the deadly disease of sin.

Pride – the old enemy. In the last lesson we began to investigate why so many people never find the Lord. We discovered that stubbornness keeps many away from the Saviour. This week we have discovered other enemies – pride and superiority. Very few Pharisees ever became Christians, because they thought they were too good to need a Saviour. The Bible always warns against pride. Will it ruin your life also, and blind you to your great need of forgiveness?

Hardness and Hate (14)
Jesus Heals on the Sabbath

Mark 3.1-6

Aim: To demonstrate that many 'religious' people are further from the kingdom of God than irreligious people. To teach the children to discern false religion and to appreciate, by contrast, the Lord.

Teachers' Introduction

Many children are hindered from seeking the Lord because of the kind of religious services so often presented to them at school and on television. They react, quite rightly, against the formalism and hypocrisy which parades itself in the name of God. If we have any real concern for their souls we should be, like our Saviour, angry and grieved. Like Him we should be prepared to expose these false representatives of the Lord.

Lesson Outline

In order to convey to the class that the outward goodness of the Pharisees only disguised the evil of their hearts, we suggest the following approach to the lesson.

Describe the events of the Sabbath morning in Capernaum. Many people set out for the synagogue, amongst them the scribes and Pharisees angling for attention in the following ways:

(1) They were not content to dress like others. They wore religious garb (robes, phylacteries, etc).

(2) They were anxious to display their strict observance of the numerous Sabbath 'bye-laws' which their groups had invented and followed over the years. They kept these meticulously (walking only so many steps, carrying only a certain weight, etc).

(3) They exhibited their devoutness by stopping to pray on street corners, and taking the front seats in the synagogue.

Genuine? Ask the class what was really passing through their minds? Were they thinking of God's Word? Were they anxious to put their lives right before entering His house? Or were they out to impress other people and to convince themselves that they were superior people and righteous in God's sight?

The plan. Disclose that something even worse was going on. They were inventing a scheme to trap the Lord Jesus and to make Him appear a common Sabbath-breaker before the people. How?

(1) First, they intended to use God's house and a service of worship to enact this scheme.

(2) They planned to use a handicapped person as the focal point of their cunning.

(3) They were too cowardly to challenge Jesus directly, but planned to use this underhanded method to 'stab Him in the back'.

Outline their scheme. The man with the withered hand was deliberately watched. The Pharisees anticipated that his serious handicap would draw out Jesus' characteristic compassion. But as soon as a healing was performed, they would make charges of Sabbath-breaking. Describe how they anticipated the humiliation of their enemy in the eyes of all the people.

A lifeless limb restored. Describe what actually happened:

(1) The Lord Jesus read their thoughts and knew their plan.

(2) Although He sensed the danger, He did not allow His compassion for the man to be set aside.

(3) Instead of quibbling over minor details, He set before the congregation the grand principles of God's law – 'Is it right to do good on the Sabbath day?'

(4) The simplest member of the congregation saw the point; the Pharisees remained silent and sullen.

(5) Jesus was angry that men who pretended to represent His heavenly Father could be so hard and callous.

(6) Without waiting further, Jesus healed the man's hand. He asked him to do something impossible – to stretch out his hand (the trouble was that he could not do this). But as the man *attempted* to do so in obedience to Christ's command, the hand was healed – a lesson on faith.

(7) Describe the different reactions: the man was so glad to have his right hand (children know its value) restored, the common people rejoiced, but the scribes and Pharisees consulted with the politicians to destroy Jesus. Even this miracle could not convince them or soften their hearts.

What do we learn?

(1) Stubborn pride usually leads to something worse. This week's lesson shows the Pharisees out to kill the Lord. Will we also become His enemies?

(2) Not all church-goers are true believers. If people are more interested in what they wear to church, how they walk to church, where they sit in church – beware! If a priest dresses up in ornate and costly robes, and performs acts of ritual and pageantry in a magnificent cathedral, but shows no obedience to the Bible – even displaying boredom as he reads the prayers – then ask: Is he a modern Pharisee or an earnest believer? Tell the class that through church history, God's real servants – men such as Luther, Tyndale, Wesley and Spurgeon – have found opposition from such religious leaders.

(3) All must look at their own hearts. Do we come to Sunday School but harden our hearts to the message of the Gospel? Can we hear of Jesus' death for sinners and coldly shrug it off? One of the Lord's greatest enemies was one of His disciples. Let us look at our hearts!

Think of what we have learned about Jesus in this lesson:–

(a) His concern for the man with the withered hand could not be diverted even under these circumstances.

(b) He was willing to reason with and to help the scribes and Pharisees even though He knew their hostility and hypocrisy.

(c) He hated sin. He refused to compromise and seek the favour of the authorities.

Urge the class to soften their hearts to the Saviour and seek His love and forgiveness, while they may. If they have never before been touched by the Saviour's love at Calvary, suggest they ask the Lord to melt their hearts:

> Give me a sight, O Saviour,
>   Of Thy wondrous love to me,
> Of the love that brought Thee down to earth,
>   To die on Calvary.
>
> Oh make me understand it,
>   Help me to take it in,
> What it meant to Thee, the Holy One,
>   To bear away my sin.

Hypocrisy (15)
Jesus Condemns the Pharisees

Mark 7.1-23; see also Matthew 23

Aim: To show the children the danger of ever relying on an outward show of goodness when all is wrong inside.

Teachers' Introduction

At first sight this vital lesson might seem a difficult one, but with a little care it can be fascinating. It will be greatly enhanced with the preparation of a few visual aids to make the points clear to the youngest children. We see the importance which Jesus attached to making these matters plain. Much of Mark's Gospel is devoted to His treatment of the Pharisees and scribes. Following His example, we must invest effort in warning the budding hypocrites in our classes.

Lesson Outline

Ask the class members what their idea of sin is. Show them

some newspaper cuttings headlining various obvious sins, and suggest that many people feel proud of themselves, and satisfied with their 'goodness' because they are not involved in the more brutal and extreme crimes.

Remind the class of the Pharisees and scribes who considered themselves vastly superior because they not only avoided *open sin* but practised *outward goodness*. Surprise the class by stating firmly that the Lord Jesus said that the Pharisees and scribes would not go to Heaven *(Matthew 5.20; and 23.15)*; neither shall we unless we are much better than they were. Go on to pose the question – Why did Jesus say that these 'good' people would go to hell? Is it possible that we too shall go to hell, even though we consider ourselves quite good?

Outward not inward. This lesson explains why the Pharisees were all wrong. The things which mattered to them were – *outward, not inward (Mark 7.1-5, 14-15)*. For a visual aid find something like a fine china cup the outside of which can be admired for its beauty, but which, when turned, is shown to be full of dirt or mud or mould. Describe the meticulous ritual which the Pharisees and scribes went through before they ate any food. Tell the class how they condemned Jesus' disciples for omitting this strict performance.

Contrast their ideas with the teaching of Jesus. He said that the things which make a man dirty and stained in God's sight are not the things which go into him, such as food and drink, but the things which come out of him, such as thoughts, words or behaviour.

Help the class to see how ridiculous it was for the Pharisees to fuss over the number of times their *hands* were washed when all the time their *hearts* were full of pride, selfishness, deceit, malice and other evils. God was far more interested in their hearts than their stomachs! Having seen this to be the case with the Pharisees, ask the class what the Lord sees when He looks into their hearts.

Show how like the Pharisees we are. We like to look good, wear fashionable clothes, own splendid bikes, cars, equipment etc, and forget that all the time God is looking within, searching for a grateful, unselfish heart, an honest tongue, and a clean mind. Jesus went on to compare the Pharisees with whitewashed tombs, shining white on the outside and full of foul, stinking bodies inside (*Matthew 23.27-28*).

Tell the class that God looks far deeper than the outward show they manage to put on for other people. He sees the *real* person. The Bible tells us that though we may consider ourselves rich and better than others, God sees our souls as wretched, miserable, poor, blind and naked (*Revelation 3.17*).

Little things, not big things (*Mark 7.9-13; Matthew 23.23-24*). For a visual aid a bunch of mint and a charity badge will help illustrate the points. The Pharisees were very particular over the smallest of things. Mint is almost a weed. It grows everywhere, yet they were so anxious to show how perfect they were that they even gave tithes of this. They probably counted every leaf and paid the amount necessary to keep their law. Yet all the time they may have had a sick parent, miserable and desperately in need. They would excuse their neglect of the old person by boasting of their devotion to God's law!

There are many people today who are very proud of themselves because they give 50p to charity while they spend big sums on the things they want for themselves. God is interested in our hearts and lives, and when we truly hand these over to Him, He remakes us, so that He can bless us and walk with us.

Religion, not God (*Mark 7.6-8; Matthew 23.1-12*). For a visual aid, pictures of cathedrals, high altars, candles, etc, will be useful. Describe how the Pharisees and scribes were very, very pleased with their religion. They loved to wear special religious clothing which marked them out from others, and they were eager to perform all kinds of elaborate religious ceremonies, but when the Lord looked for the marks of real godliness these were totally missing. The final test arrived when God's own Son came to live among them. The Pharisees found nothing in common with Him. On the contrary they were immediately filled with hatred towards everything He did and said.

Teach your children that they must never imagine that God will accept them because they go through some outward religious ceremony. Being christened or baptised has never saved anyone. These things do not bring about conversion. Going to church services does not guarantee that we become true Christians. Ask the children what makes the difference between an unconverted church-goer and a truly converted one. Outward acts of religion do not save souls. A true Christian is one who has been changed *within*, and has genuinely come to know God.

Crowds, not souls *(Matthew 23.13-15)*. The Pharisees liked to have a large following. They were anxious that the synagogues should be packed to hear them and they went to great lengths to ensure that this happened. But having done this they were not bothered about showing people how to know God. They did not want to see a marked change in the lives of the people, or any kind of spiritual rebirth.

Apply this to our situation. Many religious leaders want people to listen to their opinions about politics or social matters, but they are not concerned to preach God's Word or see real conversions. The truth is that these kinds of religious leaders do not know God themselves.

Close the lesson by encouraging the children in this way. Tell them that the Lord would be far more pleased if one ordinary child turned to Him, truly sorry for his or her sin, genuinely wanting His forgiveness, and willing to serve Him, than He would be with a cathedral full of proud people whose sole concern was how good they appeared in the estimation of others.

Dishonesty (16)
Jesus Arrives in Jerusalem

Mark 11.15-19. (See also Mark 14.10-11, 53-65; 15.1-15, 31; and 12 28-34.)

Aim: To show the ultimate sin of the scribes and Pharisees in crucifying the Son of God, and to give an example of the magnitude of God's mercy in His willingness to convert even this kind of sinner.

Teachers' Introduction

Many children are vaguely familiar with the main events

surrounding the crucifixion. This lesson aims to bring real interest to the scene by concentrating on the part which the religious leaders played. We have already seen the full range of sinfulness of these men. We have described their closed minds, stubbornness, self-righteousness, hatred and hypocrisy. In this closing section of the series we shall see their utter dishonesty as they are exposed by the Lord as having made the Temple a 'den of thieves'.

Lesson Outline

Open the lesson by describing the tumultuous reception from the crowds as Jesus reached Jerusalem.

Christ in the Temple. Explain that in previous lessons we have seen how the scribes and religious leaders travelled north to investigate and criticise the Lord Jesus. They loved to cultivate the image of being learned religious leaders, devoted to the work of God. On this occasion everything was reversed, for the Lord Jesus came to see and investigate their work. This time He journeyed south to the Temple to 'inspect' what they were doing.

Describe the sight which confronted Jesus and His disciples as they entered the Temple and saw its large interior looking more like a market place. Pigeons and other animals were being offered for sale as sacrifices at highly inflated prices. Describe, too, the tables where Roman currency was exchanged for Temple money, the exchange rate being fixed criminally in favour of the Temple authorities.

Now it was plain for all to see that far from being God-fearing, innocent and devout, these religious leaders were out to line their pockets. The extortion once practised by Matthew and his friends seemed mild in comparison with the racketeering which these men carried out in the name of God. Many Jews shrugged off this basic dishonesty, but the Lord Jesus was filled with indignation and anger when He saw His Father's house used for such corrupt things.

Jesus' anger and action. Although He knew that His actions would cause these Jewish leaders to hate Him, Jesus went straight into the Temple and drove out those who were buying and selling. He even overturned the tables of those who sold animals, and He publicly accused the religious leaders of turning God's house into a den of thieves.

Obviously, the Lord must have employed some of His 'concealed' reserves of divine power and authority to do such a thing without opposition. It seems as though the crooks and money-changers were totally unable to resist His commands.

Imagine the effect of these words and actions! Today, journalists would only dare to make such allegations and exposures under the protection of a powerful press. All the hatred and jealousy harboured in the hearts of the religious leaders was inflamed and they began to plan Jesus' destruction. Only one thing held them back – the Lord's popularity with the people.

Before continuing, remind the class solemnly that God's attitude to sin and hypocrisy is still the same. He does not regard it with the indifference which we display, but He hates sin, and will one day judge the world and send into everlasting punishment all who go through life unrepentant.

Dirty tricks. (Teachers of younger classes may not have time to include these two sections. They should proceed to the 'Gospel conclusion'.) Describe the full horror of the priests' sin as they used Judas to inform them of Jesus' whereabouts. As priests served as judges they were able to manipulate the trial of Jesus too. It was held at dead of night with only false witnesses to speak. Determined to condemn Jesus, they accused Him of the sin of blasphemy. He could not and would not refute the charge of calling Himself 'Christ, the Son of God'. They therefore gave the verdict of guilty, and sentenced Him to death.

Pilate and Calvary. Finally, describe how these so-called religious men petitioned Pilate for Jesus' death claiming that He had incited the people to rebel against Caesar. Picture their frenzy as Pilate hesitated, and how the priests resorted to stirring up the crowd to help get their way. Even Pilate could see that only envy and hatred motivated them.

Not satisfied with seeing Jesus pinned to the cross between two blatant criminals, the priests gave vent to their hatred by mocking the dying Son of God with their sarcastic taunts – *He saved others; He cannot save Himself.* These words must surely echo in their ears through all their eternity of hell, as they realise that had they listened to Him, they would have found that He was willing to save them.

A Gospel conclusion. Turn to *Mark 12.28-34* and close the lesson by telling the class that the Lord is always just and fair. He judges us individually and never overlooks the earnest efforts of a seeker whatever his or her background. So many of the scribes and Pharisees were evil and antagonistic that it would have been easy for Jesus to condemn them all. Yet here we read of a scribe for whom Jesus held out great hope.

This scribe came to Jesus with a genuine question. (The now familiar comment, *that they might accuse Him,* is not made in this man's case.) The scribe showed some heartfelt agreement with Jesus' answer, recognising that the opinions of his colleagues were wide of the mark. He grasped that love for God was far more important than anything else.

Now, while this scribe was not yet a believer, even his seemingly small amount of interest and sincerity was noted and welcomed by the Lord. Indicate the kindness of the Saviour to your class. Show them that people cannot make *themselves* perfect in God's sight, as the Pharisees claimed. Only if we admit our sinfulness, and see our need of mercy and conversion, will the Lord listen to our prayers. Then He changes the hardest heart and washes away all our sin. He loves to hear us pray like this:

> *And yet I want to love Thee, Lord:*
> *Oh, light the flame within my heart,*
> *And I will love Thee more and more*
> *Until I see Thee as Thou art!*

Once we pray such words genuinely, the Lord will begin to teach us wonderful things. He will show us that all *our* pride, deceit, hatred and selfishness was laid on Him and He bore the punishment due to us.

As we begin to understand these things we shall be filled with shame and overwhelmed with love for a Saviour Who gave His life for proud sinners like us. We shall long to please Him. To love Him with all our heart and soul and mind and strength will no longer be an impossible duty, but we shall want to serve Him. We shall discover that the Lord Himself has removed our cold, stony hearts and replaced them with hearts which feel and know Him.

How Can We Go to Heaven? (17)
The Temple Curtain Torn from Top to Bottom

Mark 15.38; Hebrews 9

Aim: To show that there is only one way to Heaven and to explain simply and clearly how the death of the Lord Jesus Christ is the only hope for sinners. To warn that unless we trust in the Saviour's death for us, we shall bear the punishment for our own sin in hell.

Teachers' Introduction

Nothing is so wonderful as to explain to young children the way in which the Saviour redeemed His people and opened the way to Heaven. Modern liberal influence has convinced many Christians that children cannot understand a concept such as the atonement. Yet it is the glory of the Gospel that even the youngest, simplest child can grasp the way of forgiveness. Doing wrong, being truly sorry and seeking forgiveness are part of daily living for the youngest child and the Saviour condemned His disciples for withholding His kingdom from such. The following notes go to some length to suggest a way of expressing these truths in a form which is simple and plain even for young children.

There are two mistakes to avoid:–

(1) *Complication.* Avoid going into elaborate details of the ritual and design of the Temple. The Lord intended these pictures to simplify, not confuse.

(2) *Arminianism.* Sometimes even those who are convinced of reformed doctrines adopt a very Arminian presentation when teaching the Cross to children.

Before teaching this lesson, give careful thought to the words to be used, the method of expression.

Lesson Outline

Surprise the class by explaining that very many people will not go to Heaven. God made this clear in the picture language of the Temple. The Holy of Holies (which He touched with His presence) was separated from the rest of the Temple by a large and heavy veil which said in effect, *No Entry*. A veil is used to hide away and cordon off some precious object to protect it from prying eyes and possible damage. People who lived before Jesus came were thus taught that sin cannot enter into God's presence. No sinner can approach God unless his sin is somehow taken away.

This means that no unforgiven person can ever go to Heaven. This raises some serious questions. Why can't we go to Heaven? If God is love, surely He will not send us to hell? Is our sin bad enough to exclude us from happiness throughout eternity?

(1) Use illustrations to explain that God is pure and holy. Nothing can remain pure even if only the tiniest drop of impurity is added to it. Immediately the whole is contaminated. (For younger classes a drop of black ink mixed with a glass of pure milk will illustrate the point.) If any sin were allowed to enter Heaven, God would no longer be pure and holy; Heaven itself would be spoiled. God cannot and must not allow unforgiven sinners into Heaven. The veil of the Temple represents the closed door of Heaven.

(2) God is so pure that sin cannot survive in His presence. No one can see God and live, the Bible teaches us. Just as heat destroys bacteria, so the holiness of God destroys sin. Should a sinner ever enter God's presence he would instantly perish. Darkness cannot live alongside light. As soon as the light shines, the darkness must go. In this world we can hide our sin and shame to some extent, but once we step into God's presence it will be exposed and the unwashed sinner will surely die.

How then can anyone go to Heaven? This problem has concerned God more than us, and it is He, not us, Who has found a solution. A veil suggests a *passable* barrier. We have all heard of pictures and plaques being unveiled. Unlike a brick wall, a veil is a temporary barrier. It indicates that there is a *possibility* of a breakthrough. So God promised the believers of the Old Testament, and those who love Him today, that He would find a way to bring us to Heaven.

How? It was at the very moment when the Lord Jesus Christ died on the cross that the Temple veil was torn from top to bottom. What did that mean? It meant that the only way for us to know God, to have our sins forgiven and to be sure of a home in Heaven, was through the death of the Saviour on the cross.

What happened on the cross? What took place when the Lord was crucified? Perhaps you always thought it was sad that Jesus should die, and you were puzzled that God should allow such a thing to happen. If this is what you thought, listen carefully because something very great and very wonderful was happening when the Lord died on Calvary's cross. This was no accident. It was planned before the world began. God realised that man would sin and be sent out of the garden made for him. Yet God had compassion upon us and in great love He longed to bring sinners back to Himself. So the Lord Jesus, the second Person of the Godhead, volunteered to come into the world in order to save us. How?

Explain how the Lord Jesus, Who had never sinned and Who should never have died, willingly agreed to give His life for all those who would be forgiven. He allowed wicked men to nail Him to the tree, and instead of escaping or calling the angels to rescue Him, He underwent the shame and agony of that terrible death so that He might save many people. As He hung upon the cross, His heavenly Father laid on Him all the guilt of His people – a punishment far greater than the physical pain.

When you become a Christian you know that every one of your sins was laid on Jesus, and He bore all the punishment for you. Unforgiven people will go to hell and suffer the consequences and pain of their own sin, but forgiven people know that Jesus carried all that pain and suffering for them in the space of a few hours as He hung on the cross.

Redeemed. Even God's own Son knew how it felt to be 'shut out' from His Father, to be forsaken by God Himself (*Mark 15.34*). Though exceedingly terrible for Jesus at that time, this was the greatest moment of history, for the Lord Jesus there made a way back to God for all who would believe and trust Him. He unlocked the gate of Heaven to let us in. Because the punishment of their sin was borne by Him, sincere seekers can be declared clean and free by the Lord as soon as they repent. God is able to welcome us into Heaven because our sins are gone, and we may therefore be regarded

White card

Blue card

Glue

White

Blue

OPENING THE WAY INTO GOD'S PRESENCE FOR ALL WHO TRUST IN HIM

"There was no other good enough to pay the price of sin He only could unlock the gate of Heaven and let us in."

TORN FROM TOP TO BOTTOM

AS THE LORD JESUS DIED

10"

Blue

6"

12"

6"

Take a large sheet of Blue card, size as shown, and fold it in three, so that the two outside pieces meet in the middle. Glue white card in the centre as shown. Print the words as above.

THE VEIL OF THE TEMPLE

veiling the Holy of Holies

from Sinners

Fold the blue card in and draw the temple veil on the front. Write these words on the veil.

Unfold as lesson proceeds

VA 4 – Visual Aid for use with Lesson 17 – 'How Can We Go to Heaven?'

as though we are pure and clean.

The cost of bearing away sin was very great, but the Lord was willing to pay the price and secure our forgiveness with His own precious blood. He was able to endure the shame and the agony due to us in order to rescue us from hell. Like a mother who willingly makes sacrifices to help her children, so the Saviour gladly laid down His life knowing His death would give us life. He redeemed us not with silver or gold, or pounds, but with something far more precious – His own blood.

Will you go to Heaven? Many people know that Jesus died, but still do not go to Heaven. Will you be among those who knew how to be forgiven but never asked God to save them?

The only way to Heaven. Remember there is only this one way to Heaven. The veil was not torn when Jesus was born, wonderful though that day was. Neither was it torn as Jesus taught His wonderful parables, or performed those great miracles. It was torn as He *died*. You can sing Christmas carols every year and never go to Heaven! You could know the parables and other parts of the Bible by heart, and still not go to Heaven! Some people live in monasteries and say endless prayers to Mary, yet these things will not get them to Heaven.

The only way to be certain of Heaven is to realise that all your hope depends on the Lord Jesus Christ and what He did for you at Calvary. If you are to become a real Christian, you will have to realise what a sinner you are – how unfit you are to ever meet God. You will have to admit that however good you try to be you will never be clean enough for Heaven. Then you will have to turn your gaze to the Cross where Jesus died and realise that He died there for such a sinner as you are.

It may even make you cry when it dawns on you that God's only Son was bearing away your sin. There can only be one explanation and that is just what the Bible tells us – that He loved us and gave Himself for us. The moment you recognise His amazing love and your own unworthiness and ask Him to wash away your sin, then He will embrace you and welcome you as His own child.

Knowing the Lord. You will not have to wait until you reach Heaven to know you are a member of God's family, one of His very own. From the moment that you repent you will be able to speak to the Lord God as your heavenly Father and Friend, and you will want to live for Him and experience His blessing day by day.

In this series we have learned a lot about the ugliness of sin and hypocrisy. The way to avoid becoming a 'scribe' or 'Pharisee' is to see yourself as God sees you. As teachers we long to see you turning to the Saviour, very earnestly and very seriously, and finding Him ready to forgive and save you. We shall soon know that He has converted and changed you, because you will be so different, so glad, so pleased.

When you think of the Lord Jesus dying on Calvary's cross, and you see in your imagination His arms spread wide, remember that by making this sacrifice He was inviting *you* to find forgiveness and pardon.

Visual Aid

VA 4 (see page 85) is an easy-to-make visual aid which will explain the picture language of the Temple veil.

Series 4
Acts (Part I)
Highlights from
THE CONVERSION &
PREACHING JOURNEYS OF PAUL

18 – Saul's Conversion
A proud, self-righteous Pharisee sets off to persecute Christians, but on the road to Damascus there is a very unexpected turn of events. Within days Saul is willing to lose everything of which he was so proud, in exchange for knowing Christ and His righteousness. From now on he will be willing to go anywhere and suffer anything in order to take the Gospel message to all who will hear and believe, not only to Jews, but also to large numbers of Gentiles.

All Christians have experienced a deep, humbling and life-transforming conversion. Have you?

19 – The Conversion of Lydia at Philippi
The Lord opens the heart of a wealthy business woman in this busy city. Not only is her life changed but her home is put at the disposal of the Lord. All who have truly experienced the Lord's saving love are ready to give themselves and their possessions to Him.

20 – The Conversion of the Jailor
What must I do to be saved? – the all-important question everyone should be asking. The jailor of Philippi receives the answer to this question in the middle of the night, following

an earthquake and his attempted suicide. Listen for the answer as carefully as he did.

21 – Paul Visits Athens
Throughout history the Greeks have been admired for their architecture and learning. In this lesson Paul visits Athens in the days of its splendour and glory. But most of its mighty men were too infatuated by their own wisdom to see the glory of the Lord Jesus and His Cross.

It is the same today. Men, women and children are too busy and preoccupied with the fleeting pleasures and achievements of this world to consider seriously the message from their Creator. Don't make the same mistake.

22 – A Riot at Ephesus
When Paul visits Ephesus, books worth 50,000 pieces of silver are burned, hundreds of people turn to the Lord, and the city silversmith fears he will go out of business. Soon a near riot is in progress.

Becoming a Christian always involves parting with this world's gods, and often this makes us unpopular. Far better to know the friendship of the Lord than the friendship of the world.

23 – Paul Before Felix
A ruthless Roman governor trembles as Paul, his prisoner, fearlessly spells out God's message to him. Soon he can stand it no longer and sends Paul away, thinking only of monetary gain. How sad when boys and girls understand and feel the Gospel message, yet brush it aside for the sake of enjoying the next few hours. How dangerous too!

24 – Onesimus
Paul is now under house-arrest in the world capital of those days – Rome. Despite his chains he is able to help a runaway slave find the Saviour, and we are able to read the letter which he wrote to Onesimus' former master, Philemon.

Christians always long to tell others 'the way back to God from the dark paths of sin'. You too either need to hear or to tell this message.

25 – Revision
A whistle-stop tour of the towns and people we have

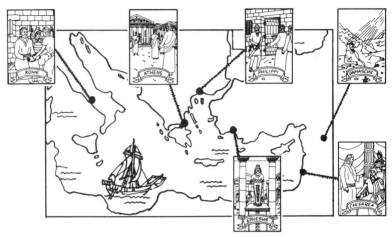

Copy the following drawings for the series of lessons on Paul. Draw a large map and as the lessons proceed attach a length of thread to locations as above.

VA 5 – *Visual Aid for use with lessons on 'The Conversion and Preaching Journeys of Paul.*

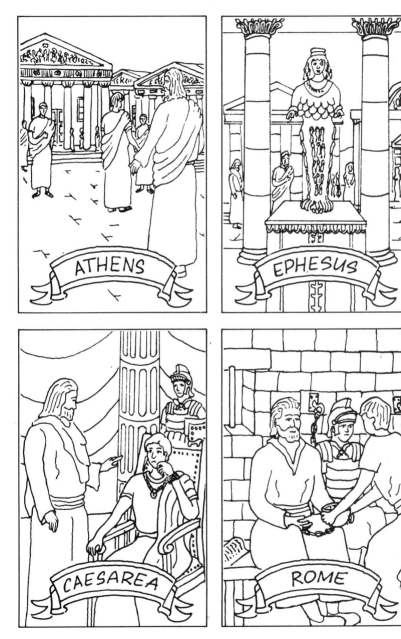

ATHENS

EPHESUS

CAESAREA

ROME

learned about in recent weeks. How much do you remember? Have their experiences had any effect on your life?

Teacher's Introduction to Series

Sunday School notes often present Paul's journeys in great detail. The emphasis is placed on the geography and history of the area. Our chief concern is to present evangelistic material which will be of soul-saving value to our children. We have, therefore, been very selective in our choice of material, simply using those incidents which answer our purpose.

Teachers are encouraged to use maps, background pictures and photographs (eg: of the Acropolis), but to limit their use to provide 'perspective'. Instead of confusing the children with a mass of complex geographical detail, we aim to present the more memorable 'salvation' incidents and events.

Visual Aid

VA 5 (see pages 90-91) is the visual aid suggested for use throughout this series. It is based on a simple map which may be added to each week with a drawing to illustrate the town featured in the lesson.

Saul's Conversion (18)

Acts 9.1-22; see also Philippians 3.1-11

Aim: To show what a profound change takes place in a person's life and heart when the Lord converts the soul.

Lesson Outline

Introduction. Ask the class how a person can be converted. Does becoming a Christian only mean that we believe there was a person named Jesus Who came to forgive sins? Does it only mean that we add Sunday School or church attendance to our weekly programme?

Tell how the lessons on which we are about to embark teach that becoming a Christian is the biggest change that can possibly take place in anyone's life. We begin today by learning how the Lord transformed the proud, self-righteous Saul into a devoted and humble servant of the Lord Jesus.

Proud of the law. Describe how the young Saul was born in Tarsus and grew up to be a zealous Jew. As a boy he learned the ten commandments and the complicated ceremonial laws. But instead of realising (as God intended) that he could not keep these great laws, and that he was a sinner in God's sight, Saul grew up proudly imagining that he *was* keeping the law, and that he stood blameless before God.

Proud of being a Jew. As he grew older he became very proud of being a Jew. Instead of valuing all the things he was taught, and wanting the whole world to know that the God of the Bible is the only true and living God, he boasted that he belonged to an 'aristocratic' race, and that God had no dealings with common Gentiles. He took the view that when the Messiah came, He would come to lift the Jewish nation into a position of political supremacy. Saul never saw the need of a Saviour to bear away his sin.

Proud of religious ritual. As soon as Saul was old enough he went to the school of the Pharisees in Jerusalem under the leadership of the great Professor Gamaliel. Younger children can picture his pride as he donned his pharisaical robes and set off for the great city of David. Here Saul learned the details of Jewish ritual and law, and studied the sacrifices daily offered in the Temple.

Instead of allowing these to teach him the importance of a great atonement to be made by the promised Saviour, as God intended, Saul put great trust in the sacrifices themselves and was meticulous in their observance. He was certain that these sacrifices would place him in very good standing in God's eyes.

His reaction to the Gospel. Describe Saul's horror when he came to hear the Christian teaching which was flooding Jerusalem at the time of his studies there. Enthusiastic Christians were proclaiming that the Saviour promised by God in the Scriptures had come in the person of Jesus of Nazareth. But instead of welcoming Him, the Jewish leaders had handed Him over to Pilate and demanded His crucifixion.

The Christians told everyone that God had raised Jesus

from the dead, as He was the Christ, and that His death ended all the Jewish sacrifices for it was the great sacrifice which these merely pictured. Thousands of Jews had already repented of their sin and come to know Christ as their Saviour. Saul was furious.

(a) He did not want to admit that he had fallen far short of God's righteous law and needed a Saviour.

(b) He did not want to share God's love with the Gentiles who he so despised. Yet already the Christians were insisting that Christ had died for *all* who believe in Him, both Jews and Gentiles.

(c) He was infuriated by the Christian teaching that Jesus, as the Lamb of God, had made the perfect sacrifice on the cross and that no more animal sacrifices and ceremonies would be necessary.

Saul convinced himself that Christians, far from representing God, were His enemies, and all his religious passion was stirred against them. He gladly consented as one of their leaders, Stephen, was stoned to death. Yet as he watched and listened to his dying speech, something pricked his heart, which he refused to consider but could not forget.

He spared no pains in arresting and imprisoning as many believers as possible. When news came that many of the persecuted Christians had left Jerusalem and were spreading the Gospel in the towns and cities where they had fled, Saul volunteered to be the chief official to hunt them down and arrest them. He was determined to stamp out their heresy. Determined to arrest many and have them put to death, he travelled to Damascus.

The journey to Damascus. Relate the events of Saul's journey to Damascus. Everyone (before conversion) rejects the Gospel message as Saul did, and the Lord has to intervene and speak to us personally, as He did with Saul. Saul was stopped in his tracks and addressed by the Lord Himself. He was brought to his knees and made to acknowledge the existence and authority of the Lord Jesus.

Having submitted himself to God, he was led blind to Damascus, where he poured out his heart to God in prayer. We know from his epistles the changes which had to be made in his life. He had to undergo such a transformation that he

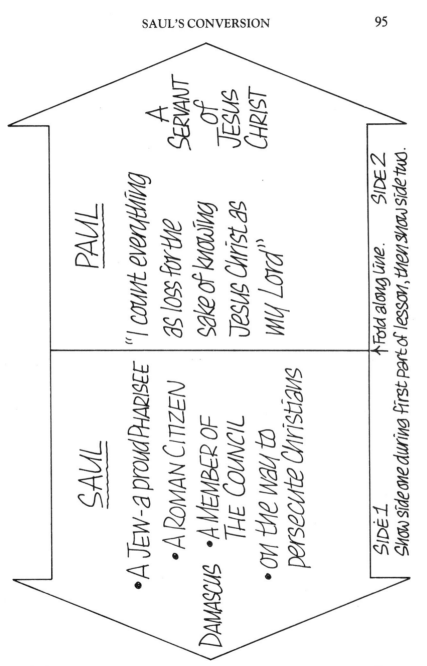

SIDE 1
Show side one during first part of lesson, then show side two. **SIDE 2**

Fold along line.

SAUL
- A JEW - a proud PHARISEE
- A ROMAN CITIZEN
- A MEMBER OF THE COUNCIL
- on the way to DAMASCUS to persecute Christians

PAUL
"I count everything as loss for the sake of knowing Jesus Christ as my Lord"

A SERVANT of JESUS CHRIST

VA 6 – Visual Aid for use with Lesson 18 – 'Saul's Conversion'.

described it later as being created all over again. All the old things which he had believed and trusted in had to be thrown away, and he had to turn to the Lord with all his heart (*2 Corinthians 5.17*).

(a) He had to admit that he had broken every one of God's commands in his heart. He had to see that, far from helping him to please God, the law condemned him (see *Romans 7.7-10*).

(b) He had to acknowledge that all his good deeds and religious ceremonial were as filthy rags in God's sight. The only way to be put right in God's eyes was to believe that the Lord Jesus had died in his place at Calvary. His only hope must be in Christ (see *Romans 3.9* and *20-26*).

(c) He had to forget his proud ambition to become a great and respected Jewish leader. It would be necessary for him to join himself to the despised and hated followers of Jesus. Surprisingly, the Lord had determined that he would be His chief messenger to the Gentiles, for whom he had shown so much contempt. Instead of a life of honour and fame he was told how much he must suffer for the name of Jesus.

Saul did not struggle against the call of the Lord once he had seen Jesus. He was then ready to surrender utterly and completely. To know the Lord came to mean more to him than anything else (*Philippians 3.8-9*), and from then onwards he was willing to endure anything for his Saviour, as we shall see in the following weeks.

What does conversion mean to us? Ask the class if they realise that conversion is a very dramatic event.

(a) Perhaps they come to Sunday School feeling quite pleased with themselves, thinking they are being quite good to come, and therefore better than other children.

(b) They too must face the Lord and realise that in fact they are enemies of God and have sinned against Him. We hope that some will sense that the Lord is speaking to them at Sunday School, calling them to give up their rebellion and turn to the Lord Jesus Who loved them and gave Himself for them.

(c) Once they see how wrong they have been, they will be amazed at the kindness and patience which the Lord has shown them. Realising His love for them, they will be willing and glad to put Him above everything else in their lives and become His willing servants too.

Visual Aid

The 'arrow' diagram (VA 6, page 95) will help present in a graphic and memorable way the main points of the lesson.

The Conversion of Lydia at Philippi (19)

Acts 16.10-15

Aim: To describe the manner and effects of Lydia's conversion in such a way that children will understand how they too may be converted, and the difference that this will make to their lives.

Lesson Outline

Arouse the children's interest by explaining that this lesson tells how Paul, Silas and Luke arrived for the first time in Europe where the first person to be converted was a woman named Lydia.

A business woman. The twentieth century is not the first in which women have been prominent in industry and trade. Lydia was a business woman who specialised in selling purple cloth. Her home town was Thyatira, in Asia Minor, which was famous for its purple dyes. Lydia was in the business of selling these richly-coloured fabrics to the wealthy. She had probably moved from Thyatira to Philippi because this busy Roman town, situated at the 'crossroads' of Europe and Asia, was a very good place from which to operate her business.

Every Sabbath. Lydia was probably quite rich, with a large house and many servants. Whilst living in Philippi she had met with a group of Jewish women who knew the Old Testament Scriptures and who met each Sabbath day at a suitable spot beside the river, outside the town centre, to pray. Because she believed in God (though she did not *know* Him closely), Lydia joined them every week.

Remind the children how important it is to come to Sunday School every week. Soon Lydia was to learn great and wonderful things about God. If she had not met weekly with these women she might have missed the blessing.

Visitors. There were very few Jewish men in Philippi to teach this group of women, and so they were very pleased when Paul and his friends arrived on this particular Sabbath day and sat down to speak to them.

A Saviour. Tell the class what Paul would have said in his message: how the Saviour promised by the prophets had come and given Himself on Calvary for sinners. The women listened, but no one becomes a true Christian simply through listening. This message involves our hearts. We are told that the Lord opened Lydia's heart so that she responded to the things which Paul preached. List some aspects of Lydia's conversion and apply them to the class:–

(1) She was a *rich* woman, and may well have been quite proud of her wealth. But she had to turn to the Lord as a *spiritually* poor, needy sinner begging His kindness and forgiveness for her many sins. Explain that nothing that we are proud of in this world (being rich, good at games, handsome or pretty) counts with God. We all have no score at all in His book of righteousness and deserve only punishment. We depend entirely on His grace and mercy to be saved.

(2) She was a *business woman*, probably very intelligent and shrewd, but she came to see that her abilities and opinions were worthless in matters to do with the heart and soul. Lydia came to believe and trust God's Word alone. She trusted in God's method of salvation. She did not say, 'Oh, but I think I ought to be able to earn my salvation.' Nor did she say, 'Oh, but surely God will love everyone, and no one will go to hell. Therefore I can do what I like.' She threw away her own opinions and believed what God's Word said.

(3) She was used to *taking decisions* and organising her own life and those of others. Perhaps she could be rather bossy! But at this point she had to acknowledge her helplessness, and recognise that only the Lord could change her heart and life, convert her, and put *spiritual life* into her. She also had to learn that she must give up being the governor of her life, for in order to be converted we must yield to the lordship of Christ, and ask Him to be our Master. We must be ready to obey His orders.

Marks of grace. Describe the effects of Lydia's conversion:–

(1) She was baptised, publicly acknowledging her love and trust in the Lord and her joy at having her sins washed away. We should never hide the fact that we have become Christians.

(2) Other members of her household were baptised too, which tells us that her conversion was so real and plain to see, especially by those with whom she lived, that they also turned to the Saviour. Explain that if people are truly converted, their nearest and dearest immediately notice a difference in their behaviour. Christianity is not just a change of belief but a change of the whole manner of life. (It is possible for unbelieving parents to react in a hostile manner when they see the effects of conversion in their children, but whatever their reaction they will see a change.)

(3) She looked after the Lord's servants. She insisted that Paul and his fellow workers went to stay in her home. From now on everything she possessed was the Lord's, to be used in His service. We can picture her drawing room, once a luxurious room visited by elegant guests, now filled with all kinds of people (soon to include the town jailor) listening to the Gospel message. All those who believe that God's Son gave His life for them at Calvary, willingly and gladly count all their worldly possessions as His, to be used for His service.

(4) She remained faithful. Even after Paul and Silas had aroused the indignation of the town authorities and had been sent to prison, they were able to return immediately to Lydia's house after their release. By harbouring these two men, Lydia stood to become unpopular herself in a town filled with a frenzy of hatred for the apostle and his associates.

(5) She continued to support the Lord's work. Even after Paul had left Philippi, he continued to receive real help and support (gifts of money) from the church there. He referred to them as his *joy and crown*.

Use this point to teach the children that a true Christian is one who follows Jesus to the end; who, being purchased by His precious blood, is His forever.

Draw the lesson to conclusion by telling the class how the

Gospel flourished in Europe. Despite persecution, churches sprang up throughout the empire, and even in far-flung Britain there is evidence of Christian meetings in the days of Roman rule.

Visual Aid

Pictures of wealthy Roman villas are easily obtainable, together with sketches of women's costumes of that period. These will help set the scene for this lesson.

The Conversion of the Jailor (20)

Acts 16.16-40

Aim: To show the children how urgently they ought to seek the Saviour.

Lesson Outline

The jailor. Contrast Lydia, a wealthy and cultured business woman, with the rough, tough jailor of Philippi. Describe his assignment in keeping the town jail – an uncivilised prison designed to keep criminals securely, with no concessions to comfort or sanitation. Imagine the entry of the cultured and ageing Paul and Silas among the prisoners – in those days usually very disadvantaged, uneducated, coarse and bitter people.

The jailor knew that Paul was a preacher and that there was a great spirit of antagonism in the town towards him. Following an incident which threatened the livelihood of some greedy 'circus' men, Paul had been turned upon by the whole town, and even the magistrates had abandoned their impartiality and commanded that Paul and Silas should be beaten with rods in the Roman manner.

Unusual prisoners. The two preachers had been so severely beaten that their shoulders and backs were covered with bleeding gashes. Then they had been roughly bundled into the jail, where the jailor treated them very badly. The jailor seems to have caught the spirit of antagonism so rife in the town, and in spite of the age of the two men, he locked them in the stocks in the 'inner prison', which was most probably a damp cellar dug out of the earth. Such dungeons had no light or ventilation, and people left in them for any length of time soon became ill, and often died.

Paul and Silas, as missionaries, had been in Philippi for many days *(Acts 16.18)*, and during this time the spectacular incident involving the poor slave girl possessed by a demon stirred the whole town. Everyone knew who they were, and what they were preaching. The whole town turned out to shout and yell at them. The jailor also (and perhaps his family and servants) would have either heard the preaching, or heard about it, so he knew that Paul was telling people that they must all one day stand before the one true God, Who made Heaven and earth, and answer for their sin. Paul had also explained in detail how the Lord Jesus Christ had come to bear the punishment of all those who believe in Him.

A brave testimony. What must the embittered jailor have thought when he heard Paul and Silas singing psalms in the prison? What effect did it have on his antagonism and prejudice when he discovered that these men were not selfish, weak characters, fuming, cursing and feeling sorry for themselves? Perhaps he used to think that religious people were all hypocrites, who – if they came into his prison – would soon forget their God and be full of hate and misery. But to his amazement, these men turned to their God as if they really knew Him! And they prayed and sang as though He really did comfort and help them!

Perhaps the jailor began to feel how cruel, vindictive and spiteful he had been to treat these flogged and bleeding elderly men in such a terrible way. Perhaps then he began to wonder if he could ever be forgiven the sins of his life.

Two great fears. Describe the great alarm bell which rang in the jailor's soul when the earthquake shook the prison. The prisoners' chains fell from the walls and cell doors flew open. Two great fears seized the jailor.

(1) He may well have feared that almighty God was showing His anger at how His servants had been so cruelly treated. What was already touching the jailor's conscience would surely have sprung to mind in that moment!

(2) He would definitely have feared the severest punishment from the authorities if the prisoners escaped. He would certainly have suffered humiliation and destitution, perhaps

even death, even though the circumstances of their escape were outside his control.

God's mercy. To the jailor the situation seemed desperate. He lived in hard times and was not used to receiving any mercy or kindness from anyone (just as he did not give it). Thinking he was as good as dead he had drawn out his sword ready to kill himself, when Paul's voice rang through the night air. Imagine how overwhelmed he was to discover that the men he had so viciously treated only hours before were full of concern for *his* well-being. Were these preachers willing to miss their chance of escape just so that *he* could be helped? Did they care that much for his life and his soul?

The jailor was finally convinced that their God and their message were true. He threw himself down at their feet and asked that great but simple question – the question which all of us should ask – *Sirs, what must I do to be saved?* He wanted to find the forgiveness and new life which Paul and Silas preached.

A wonderful answer. Paul told him to believe on the Lord Jesus Christ. To believe in Christ means: (1) that we believe what He said about our condition – that we are lost sinners, condemned to hell because of our sin, unless we are forgiven by Him. (2) We must also believe in what He has done to save us – that He suffered and died to take *all* the punishment which we deserve, and that He did this for all those who repent of their sin. (3) We must believe His invitation: that if we come to Him and give our lives to Him, He will take us, remake our lives, and be our Lord and Saviour. (4) We must believe His promises that He will never let us go.

The jailor's hardened expression may have melted to tears as Paul described how the Saviour had suffered in order to wash away his sins. That night he believed on Jesus, repented of His sin, and became a true Christian, and so did members of his household – his wife and grown-up children and his servants perhaps. Immediately their behaviour changed, and they began to tend to the wounds of Paul and Silas. So clear was the fact that they were all deeply changed in their character, that the apostle baptised them that very night.

Saved. The jailor's transformation was sudden and wonderful. He saw that his cruel behaviour that night was a real demonstration of his foul character. It was something which lived in his heart all the time. But now he was set free from his viciousness and ugly temper. He was completely forgiven, and made a new man. Real conversion soon proved itself by actions, as we saw with Lydia. No wonder the jailor began bathing the wounds of Paul and Silas!

Remind the class that those who are converted will also experience a great change of character, and will come to walk with the Lord. Not all conversions are as sudden as the jailor's, and it may take a little time for converts to be fully certain that they have found the Lord, but what matters is that the children should begin to seek Him immediately. They should never assume that they have plenty of time to turn to God. Instead they should go as soon as possible to the Lord in prayer, asking Him to forgive them, to transform their lives and make them His, believing that the Lord Jesus loves sinners like them, and gave Himself for such.

If they believe God's promises and truly repent of all their sins it is possible that, like the jailor, they will know God's wonderful power to forgive and transform them straight away.

Visual Aid

Pictures of Paul and Silas in prison can be used. Equally useful would be the famous question of the jailor, and Paul's answer, printed on card. Encourage the class to learn these.

Paul Visits Athens (21)

Acts 17.16-34

Aim: To awaken children from their complacency and to alert them to the fact that one day they too must be judged by the one true and living God.

Lesson Outline

Athens. Explain that the apostle Paul found it necessary to travel ahead of Silas and Timothy to Athens. Describe this magnificent city, the cultural capital of the ancient world. The class might imagine that Paul would be excited to visit a place about which holiday brochures wax eloquent today. In Paul's day the buildings were not impressive ruins, but massive, beautiful stone temples adorned with dazzling marble. (We can still admire the splendid sculptures – the Elgin Marbles – displayed in the huge Duveen Gallery of the British Museum.) The streets were thronged by large numbers of people who considered themselves to be very clever. They spent their time discussing and debating the theories and philosophies of the day.

Compare this state of affairs with our own generation. We too consider ourselves to be very clever, advanced in science and technology, and we regard our forebears as comparatively simple and backward. Even young children are encouraged to air their opinions rather than to listen and learn.

Paul's sorrow and anguish. Describe Paul's reaction when, as he toured the famous city, he found it full of idols and temples dedicated to a great array of gods and goddesses. His spirit was stirred up as he thought of how the people spent their time worshipping dumb statues. To Paul it was both tragic and sickening.

Ask the class how the apostle might feel if he were to visit the streets of London or some other great city today. Would he be shocked to see that the people who boasted that they could conquer space and invent amazing computers actually spent much of their time in night clubs, pubs, discos, etc, and were hooked on drugs, alcohol and tobacco?

The Athenians revelled in news. Explain how Paul immediately set to work, preaching the Gospel first to the Jews in the synagogue and then to people in the busy market-place. Before long, word got round to the philosophers that a new teaching had come to Athens. It was not that these people were really concerned to hear Paul's message – they called him an *idle babbler* and a *proclaimer of strange deities* – but they were always curious to hear something new, and so they invited Paul to meet them.

Again teachers could point out how like the Athenians we are. People love news and gossip, even if it has to be found in episodes of *Eastenders*, *Neighbours*, or other 'soap operas'. Rather than consider the things which are really important, people fill their minds with morsels of scandal, and laugh contemptuously at anyone who tries to tell them about God, forgiveness and a life to come.

The Gospel announced. Paul was invited to stand on Mars' Hill and proclaim to the members of the Areopagus the truth about the one and only God, Who made Heaven and earth. Help the children to picture the scene. Cultured Greeks in their flowing robes, used to debating, sat and listened as Paul delivered his message.

Suggest to your class that Sunday School may sometimes seem rather serious. They must understand that whereas Christians are the happiest people on earth, yet when they speak to unbelievers they have a duty to be serious, to warn them that they need the Saviour, and to tell them how they might find Him.

Before the Second World War people took no notice of solemn warnings being made about Hitler's aggressive plans. As the war developed and millions of people lost their lives in a brutal way, many began to wish they had listened to the warnings. What sorrows might have been avoided if other nations had been ready! The Lord Jesus tells us that in hell many people will be full of remorse, wishing that they had heeded the warnings so kindly given in God's Word.

What did Paul say? Our lesson divides his message under three headings, each of which describes the Gospel message for us.

(1) A gracious message. We see that Paul was very kind to his audience. On his way to the Areopagus he had noticed among all the shrines, an altar inscribed 'To An Unknown God'. The Greeks had erected this like a lucky charm, to be on the safe side. In case there was a minor god they had overlooked or forgotten, this altar would excuse their neglect. But Paul used this inscription, like a teacher with a visual aid, to introduce his subject. He had come to tell them about the 'Unknown God'. Ask the class to consider the kindness of the Gospel message. Instead of acting in anger, God sends His servants with a message of forgiveness and invitation. Have we listened to it?

(2) A serious message. He spoke of how adults behave

like children playing with toys when they make their own gods and worship them; how there is one God Who made the world on Whom we all depend for life and breath; and of how we should all seek Him. He is not far away, Paul told them.

God tells us to seek Him early. The evidence of His creation is all around us and He expects young children to notice and learn the lessons of Heaven just as easily as adults. Pretending there is no God is a very dangerous game.

(3) **A factual message.** He gave them proof of his words by speaking of the resurrection of Jesus. This made these Athenians angry. They did not want facts – they preferred theories. The philosophers did not believe in life after death, and certainly they did not want to hear of future judgement.

Remind the class that Christians speak of facts, not opinions. The Bible is a book of events; of things which God has actually done, not theories. It is a record of the creation, the incarnation, the crucifixion and the resurrection – all historic events; things which God has done. We must never be like the foolish philosophers of Athens who did not want to hear about real things but just dreamed their lives away with theories.

Describe the reactions which Paul experienced and picture their modern equivalents:–

(1) **Some laughed.** Many of the Areopagites mocked Paul and ridiculed his message. Perhaps the preaching had pricked their hearts and their pride and the only way they could retaliate was to abuse the messenger. Suggest that many people do the same today. Rather than take the Gospel seriously they pour scorn upon it. Even young believers receive this treatment when they tell others about their faith. Warn the class against this reaction, reminding them that one day we must stand before God's judgement throne and see Him in all His power and glory. How will silly jeers and scornful remarks appear then?

(2) **Some delayed.** Explain that some of Paul's hearers were not so proud and silly. They did not immediately reject the Gospel, but said they would think about it later. Perhaps some did. However, for many this was just a polite excuse; a

cowardly way of rejecting Paul's message. Today many people, including children, refuse God in this polite but deceitful way. They do not want to come to church or Sunday School, or turn to the Lord, but they are not honest enough to say so. Instead they murmur, 'Perhaps next week.' Seeking the Lord is an urgent matter. Postponing the date may lead to our never seeking and finding Him at all.

(3) **Some believed.** The Bible does not mention that there was a church at Athens. In general the people of Athens apparently rejected God's wisdom, but there were a few who believed. Some proud members of the Areopagus acknowledged their sin, turned away from their pride and turned to the Lord, believing in Him as their Saviour. The Gospel took root in the hearts of others also, and they stayed with Paul, anxious to hear all they could.

Similarly the Lord loves to snatch children from this proud, anti-God generation and make them true Christians. Urge your class to seek Him.

Visual Aid

The preceding two sets of headings, printed clearly, will help give substance to the lesson and aid the memory. Photographs of the Acropolis are easily obtainable.

A Riot at Ephesus (22)

Acts 19.8-41; 20.17-38

Aim: To show the practical steps which the seeker must take in coming to Christ.

Lesson Outline

Capture the children's interest by describing how Paul's work caused a tremendous uproar at Ephesus. Describe how Paul's companions were seized and dragged to the town assembly by a mob of angry business men. Stirred up by the business fraternity, a vast crowd gathered and, amidst scenes of great confusion, they chanted their town slogan, 'Great is Diana of the Ephesians!' over and over again.

They managed to keep this up for about two hours before the town clerk arrived to warn them of the seriousness of their behaviour and to call the town to order. Only then did the crowd disperse. Why should Paul's preaching, which was about God's love and mercy, provoke such intense feelings?

Ephesus – the city of Diana. Describe the proud city of Ephesus. It was not a world centre like Rome or Corinth, nor could it boast the scores of gods and philosophies of Athens. But it did consider itself to be the special, guardian city of the goddess Diana. The people living in the area were highly superstitious and put their faith in magic arts. They believed that the goddess Diana had showed special favour to their city, and they rebuilt her temple in beautiful white marble.

Every family in the vicinity was frightened to live without a statue in the house (often of engraved silver). People had a superstitious regard for these.

Teachers with younger classes can describe life in a home where frightened people had to trust that Diana would protect them from diseases, fevers, earthquakes, and other hazards which were commonplace. They paid large sums of money to Diana's priests to obtain magic scrolls to protect and help them.

Tell the class that even in our scientific twentieth century, a surprising number of adults and children are still attracted to superstitious cults and religions.

A new message. Describe how Paul arrived in Ephesus. The class should know by now that he always preached first in the town synagogue. Although the Jews usually reacted violently to his message, Paul obeyed God in giving his own people the first opportunity to hear the Gospel. In addition to trying to blacken his name the Jews made every effort to destroy his good character in the eyes of the Gentile authorities.

Many Jews and Greeks came to believe in the Lord Jesus as a result of Paul's preaching in Ephesus, and he soon began to hold daily meetings in a public hall rented from a man named Tyrannus. Over a period of two years many people were converted both in Ephesus itself and in the surrounding towns and villages.

Describe how conversion affected many people in Ephesus, and how it should affect us now, basing the lesson on *Acts 19.18-19.*

(1) They believed the Gospel.

(a) They stopped believing the foolish tales associated with the lifeless Diana and recognised the one true God Who made Heaven and earth and everything in them. They believed in His own dear Son, the Lord Jesus, Who died on the cross and rose again to bring us back to God.

(b) Before we can become Christians, we also must stop believing the wrong notions which we already hold. We must stop believing in ourselves – that we are so clever, and that we shall be happy, rich and successful without God. We must stop believing that we are good enough to go to Heaven without being converted. We must stop believing that this world's entertainments and bright lights are the great things to seek, and the things that will make us happy. We must stop believing foolish, superstitious religion.

We must start believing what God says about our world, and about each one of us. We must believe in what God has done about our plight, and in what He will do for us if we repent and seek Him.

(2)They confessed and disclosed their practices.

(a) They did not repent of their sins in a vague or casual way. They listed all the evil ways and deeds of their hearts and named the wrong things of which they were ashamed.

(b) We too must be open about our sins before the Lord, and ashamed of what we have done. Teachers should emphasise that our worst crimes against God are sins of the heart – rebelling against God, refusing to believe and obey Him, and ignoring His Gospel. Sinful deeds are the *outward* crimes, due to an ugly inward state. Have we ever been deeply ashamed of our pride, selfishness, dirty thoughts or words, temper, etc?

(3) They burned their books.

(a) Having acknowledged their sin and asked God for forgiveness, they showed God that they really did want to part with the old life forever. Describe the great and unusual occasion when many believers, determined to put their sinful past behind them and turn wholeheartedly to the Lord, made a huge bonfire and brought all their magic scrolls and cult books and burned them publicly. They had paid dearly for these books (the value was estimated at many thousands of pounds), but they gladly watched the flames devour them.

(b) This is a sign of truly converted people. Those who really come to Christ not only repent, but they also yield their future lives to the lordship of Christ. They say, 'Lord Jesus, rule in my life, take me, change me, guide me, and be my Lord for ever, and in everything.' Are we willing to destroy our worldly ties?

Some people are occasionally ashamed of their sin and go to church to ask for forgiveness. But what they really want is 'relief' from an aching conscience. They have no intention of living for God the next day! Someone who truly repents also hands over his life to the Lord.

A closing plea. In closing, return to the matter of the riot. Some people were deeply resentful of the Gospel and did not like to see men and women set free from a life of fear and superstition. Demetrius, the silversmith, saw his trade dwindling and stirred up ill-feeling toward Paul and his fellow workers until the town was in an uproar.

How tragic it was that when God's messengers offered wonderful things to people (forgiveness, a totally changed life, knowing God, receiving powerful answers to prayer, and a place in Heaven for ever) there were those who clung blindly to their false god and their empty, doomed lives.

Do we cling to passing things? Do we 'worship' and serve things which have no power to bless us and save our souls?

Visual Aid

Pictures of Diana or Artemis are to be found in most Bible dictionaries. Print out the section headings from this lesson.

Paul Before Felix (23)

Acts 24 (especially verses 24-27)

Aim: To teach children that, when God convicts them of sin, they should face up to their position and seek the Saviour. They should never be like Felix, who ran away from God's warnings.

Lesson Outline

Ask the children if they have ever heard of a judge – who

possesses the power to inflict long and painful sentences upon people – trembling with fear before his prisoner. Interest them by explaining that in the course of this lesson we see Paul as a prisoner in chains, able to terrify his judge. How did this come about?

Felix – what kind of a man? Help the children to picture Felix, the Roman governor of Judea, returning with his wife to his official residence at Caesarea. This stately home had been built as a royal palace by King Herod, and no doubt the Roman governor enjoyed living there. Included in the complex of buildings was a barrack block for his troops, giving him a sense of power and security.

This particular governor especially relished all this grandeur. He had been born a slave, and had deliberately set out to gain the best for himself by whatever methods were necessary. He had risen to these heights by trampling on the lives and careers of others. The history books describe him as corrupt, cruel and greedy. He was a cheat in every aspect of his life.

Paul – the prisoner. Explain how Paul had been escorted from Jerusalem to Caesarea by two hundred soldiers, seventy horsemen and two hundred spearmen. What happened in Jerusalem to make it necessary for this enormous contingent to protect a single prisoner?

Very briefly, explain that Paul had returned to Jerusalem, and outline the events which had led to his arrest. When visiting the Temple, the Jews (some from the Asian cities he had visited) had created such an uproar that the Roman authorities had arrested Paul, partly to preserve his life.

His case had now to be tried by the governor himself. One hearing had already taken place, but the Jews had been unable to prove the charges they had brought against Paul, and so Felix had deferred the trial until the chief captain from Jerusalem could give evidence. In the meantime Paul, as a Roman citizen, had been allowed a measure of freedom within the prison quarters, and friends had been permitted to visit him and attend to his needs.

A private interview. It was not long after their arrival that the governor and his wife summoned Paul for a private audience. Drusilla was a Jewess whose father, King Herod, had persecuted Christians, and so she may have been curious to hear this man so hated by many of her people. Felix was also intrigued and wanted to see for himself what was so unusual about this man.

Paul – God's messenger. Describe how the apostle found himself standing before this regal couple in a magnificently marbled hall in the palace. This must have seemed an ideal opportunity to court their favour and win their support. Many prisoners would have used the occasion to flatter and impress. But the apostle saw Felix and Drusilla as a lost man and woman in rebellion against God, with their souls in eternal danger.

Paul fearlessly turned the conversation to matters of the heart. Soon he was convincing his judge about righteousness, self-control and judgement to come, subjects which made Felix feel very afraid.

(1) Righteousness. Paul began to show that God was not impressed by what a man *achieved*, but how he *behaved*. Felix began to feel like a wounded man. What did he know of righteousness? Had not his life been one long story of trickery, corruption and tyranny? The matter of right and wrong had hardly ever come into his reckoning.

As the darts of conscience began to take effect, Paul told Felix that all are sinners before God – *there is none righteous, not even one* – and that was the reason why God sent His Son, the Lord Jesus, to die on the cross at Calvary. He died to bear the penalty for twisted, perverted lives and to offer us the gift of His righteousness, so that vile sinners might one day walk the streets of Heaven and stand uncondemned before God's throne.

Ask the class what values they have. Do they only admire people who own big cars, win fame and adulation, or achieve great victories in sport? Remind them of God's set of values and of our total failure to appreciate and desire them, and even less to live up to them. Speak of the Saviour Who came to earn a robe of righteousness for all who see their great need and who will look to Him alone.

(2) Self-control. This subject touched a very sore spot for both Felix and his wife. Neither knew very much about self-control. If they wanted something they got it, if necessary by force. They could never say 'No' to themselves. If anyone else tried to say 'No' to them, that person suffered. Even if God said 'No' to one of Felix's whims, it made no difference – his lusts and desires had to be satisfied.

Paul explained that it was necessary for God's own Son to give His own life, in agony, bearing the penalty of sin for each person who would be forgiven. He told how when sinners repent, then their selfish, greedy hearts can be renewed. He must have told Felix that only Christ could give a weak, hopeless sinner control over himself and his lusts.

Teachers can easily show how relevant this subject is to us. We live in a world which teaches us that we must have what we want. We need never refuse our desires. If we cannot have our dreams satisfied, we feel entitled to feel sorry for ourselves and give up on life. But conversion brings a new nature which has much more self-control. How much we need that great change to be carried out in our lives.

(3) **Judgement to come.** Perhaps Felix was trying to console himself with the fact that so far he had done very well without these two qualities, when Paul proceeded to a third topic. This was even more alarming. Paul, standing in chains before the Roman ruler, reminded Felix that one day he must stand before the Judge of Heaven and earth, to be judged by Him. Nothing would be hidden; all the evidence would be available. Nor would God have 'favourites' or accept any kind of bribe.

As Paul proceeded, Felix could bear it no longer. It was as if for a moment he had stood before God's judgement and seen himself for what he really was. Inwardly the ruthless governor trembled. At that moment his heart was sufficiently touched for him to have to ask the apostle's help. Gladly would Paul have pointed him to the Saviour and shown him the way of escape.

Hardening the heart. Instead Felix hardened himself, and steeled himself against the work of God's Holy Spirit. He wanted none of this and he wanted Paul out of the way. Quickly he told the apostle to go. The most suitable lie he could muster at the time was that he would hear him another time when it was more convenient.

Warn the class against this kind of lie or deceit towards God. Urge them to face up to His kindly warnings. If they should see themselves as they really are in their sinful state – so that they feel inwardly shaken – they should not run away, but run instead to the Saviour Who can wash away even their worst sins and calm their fears.

As Felix kicked against his conscience, other thoughts quickly flooded into his mind. Could he make money from Paul? Would the apostle's friends pay a bribe in order to free him?

Never ignore God's warnings. One day, like Felix, we must appear before God's judgement seat. And then we shall wish that we had taken our Sunday School teacher seriously. We shall be filled with sorrow that when God gave us the opportunity to see our sin and repent, we threw it away and exchanged a place in Heaven for some petty earthly gain.

Onesimus (24)

Philemon, Luke 15.11-24

Aim: To use this example of a 'real life' prodigal to teach the children how runaway sinners can be rescued and restored by the Saviour.

Lesson Outline

Introduce the class to the young slave Onesimus who lived not far from Ephesus in the town of Colossae. Younger classes may picture him grumbling as he performed some chore. Explain that Onesimus may not have realised it, but he really had little to complain about. Although he was a slave, owned by a rich man, yet he had a kind master who provided good food and pleasant living quarters, and who was reasonable in his demands.

It had not always been like this. The slaves could doubtless remember the days before their master, Philemon, was converted. Then he had probably been very severe, flogging them for the smallest failure, forcing them to work long hours and caring little for their well-being.

A big change had come about in the household when

Philemon had been converted. He had heard the apostle Paul preaching the Gospel, and had come to see that he was a sinner in God's sight. He had prayed to God for forgiveness, and God had completely changed his life and character.

Wanting to be 'free'. Perhaps Onesimus had forgotten those old, hard days, and now resented the hymn-singing and Bible talks which Philemon had introduced to the household since his conversion. The young slave became dissatisfied and ungrateful. He began to dream of the world beyond, and to imagine the excitement and pleasures which were to be had elsewhere.

Then Onesimus started to take money from his master. Probably this was easy now that Philemon was a Christian. He had become more easy-going and trusting with his servants. (He probably no longer flogged those who were caught.) One night Onesimus decided the time had come for him to make his escape and he crept out of the house with his purse full of Philemon's money. He was now free – or so he thought.

Journey to a far country. Describe the kind of problems Onesimus encountered on his journey to Rome as a runaway slave and thief. Let the class picture him sleeping in barns, hiding in alleys, terrified of being arrested on suspicion of being an escaped slave. The penalties, if he were caught, were very severe.

Imagine him trying to shrug off all these difficulties and then throwing himself into all kinds of activities which, however, only stung his conscience and left him feeling sick, until he hardened himself to them. No doubt his money ran out faster than he had anticipated and he was forced to steal, and to take up the dirtiest and lowest kind of work.

Perhaps he thought it would be better in Rome. Many runaway slaves lived there. Imagine him sightseeing the magnificent buildings of the great capital – the Forum, the government buildings, the Colosseum where the great sporting events took place.

A mighty famine. This was the Rome he had heard and dreamed of. But when it came to finding somewhere to sleep, he soon discovered that the only places for people like him were tucked out of sight – grubby areas littered with drunkards and surrounded by a sinister atmosphere.

Now he was able to see the outside world for himself, but he found that it was not the glamorous, exciting, happy life he had expected. Instead he learned how rotten people could be; how greedy, cruel and heartless. Now that he was penniless no one wanted to know him. A life of crime and vice was all that was open to him. He discovered new paymasters in the underworld who cared only for themselves and took full advantage of him as a fugitive from justice.

He was now a scruffy youth with a dirty tunic, and he wore the haunted expression of a boy who knew that he looked like a fugitive slave. What sins he committed to keep alive we do not know, but we may be certain that he went very deeply into sin, and discovered that he was a 'slave' in a far worse sense than ever before.

When he came to himself. However, a change was already taking place in Onesimus. In Philemon's house he had been full of self-confidence and rebelliousness, fondly imagining that the world outside was full of freedom and pleasure. Now he was a little older and wiser. He had seen (and felt) the wickedness and hopelessness of this sinful world and its people, he was utterly miserable, and his conscience weighed heavily upon him.

We are not told in the Bible how Onesimus came in touch with Paul. Perhaps he had reached a crisis point, and having heard that Paul was in Rome, went to him in desperation. He may have heard Paul's name mentioned many times by Philemon. He knew, at least, that Christians were kind and probably he hoped Paul would give him money or help him. In total desperation he found his way to Paul's rented house. Though the apostle was under house arrest and constantly attended by a guard, he was able to see all who visited him.

His Father had compassion. Onesimus listened in a new way as Paul spoke to him. Paul did not grimace at his dirty appearance, but with great kindness he told him how God would forgive all his sins. Onesimus was very burdened with a guilty conscience. The full horror of his sin came home to him – his naivety in thinking that the world was a wonderful place; his pride in thinking he could manage better without God; his wickedness in robbing someone who had been kind to him, and all the sins of his subsequent life.

Perhaps he had heard about the Cross before, but now it really melted him down to realise that God's perfect Son had come to give His life for worthless sinners like him. The Lord Jesus had the power to wash the foulest sinners and make them clean in God's holy sight. So Onesimus prayed sincerely that God would forgive him, and the great change of conversion took place in his life.

I have sinned. Soon Onesimus was to be seen visiting Paul regularly, helping him in every way possible. He was a completely transformed person. The elderly apostle treated Onesimus as his own son and wished that he could stay in Rome with him. But they both knew that the right thing was for Onesimus to return to his master and offer to make amends for his past. Paul was sure that Philemon would forgive his former slave and welcome him back as a brother in the Lord. Although his sight was very poor, the apostle took up his pen and wrote to Philemon explaining what had happened.

Tell the class how important it is for them to face the truth about this world and their own sinfulness – how important for them to turn to the Lord and seek His forgiveness, and how important to recognise that their selfish, proud and rebellious hearts need replacing by hearts full of love for their Saviour. Urge young children to turn to the Lord early, before experiencing the bitter lessons which Onesimus had to learn.

Soon Onesimus was on his way back to Colossae carrying the letter, and wondering what Philemon would say. Paul, in that letter, mentioned that Onesimus had once been *useless* – good for nothing! But now, because God had so changed him, he was true to his name, which means 'beneficial'! His old character had been taken away, and God had made him 'new'. Do we know what it is to have such a great change take place within?

Revision (25)

Aim: To remind the children of the highlights of this series of lessons so that they are fully familiar with the main events of Paul's life and, more importantly, their spiritual lessons for us.

Lesson Outline

This series will respond well to revision.

(1) Geographically – the children can be encouraged to take a 'flight' around the Mediterranean and revisit the towns which Paul visited. Then ask carefully prepared questions about what happened at each place, eg:–

(a) Damascus. What great event took place on the Jerusalem/Damascus road? Why did Jesus say it was hard for Paul *to kick against the goads*? What was Paul prepared to count 'as loss' in order that he might know Christ? What is it that the Lord Jesus can give us that makes everything else pale into insignificance?

(b) Philippi. Name two characters known to us at Philippi. Both came to believe in the Lord Jesus Christ. What difference did it make to them? How can *we* be saved?

(c) Athens. Picture the great marbles of the Acropolis shining in the sun. Home in on the apostle Paul as he preached to the philosophers of the Areopagus. What did he tell them about the *Unknown God*? What was it that he said which turned most of them against him? Why is the resurrection so important to Christians?

(d) Ephesus. Which goddess did the people of Ephesus jealously worship? Where did the Christians meet in that town for most of the time Paul was there? As people were converted, what action did they take as they turned from superstition to the living God? What gods do we have to turn our backs on when we turn to the Lord Jesus?

(e) Caesarea. How did the apostle come to be imprisoned in the Roman governor's fortress home at Caesarea? Why did Felix tremble as Paul preached to him? What three subjects did Paul speak to him about? What will the day of judgement be like for each of us?

(f) Rome. Explain how Paul reached Rome and how he was able to witness to members of Caesar's household and speak to the Jews of the city despite being under house arrest. Tell how he wrote several of his epistles while in chains. Ask the class who Onesimus was and how he came to be in Rome. All sinners have 'run away' from the Lord – how can we return?

(2) Characteristics of conversion. An alternative method of revision would be to revise the change which came about in the chief characters of this series at their conversion:–

(a) A *proud* Pharisee became the humble servant of the Lord to the Gentiles. Outline the great changes Paul lists in *Philippians 3*, and apply them to the class.

(b) Lydia, a *rich* and successful business woman (probably haughty and grasping), became a kind and generous friend to the Lord's servants, willing to associate publicly with them in a town where they became the object of hate and vicious anger.

(c) The *stony-hearted*, brutal jailor of Philippi became polite and tender-hearted as he believed on the Lord Jesus Christ, showing every kindness to the Lord's servants.

(d) Fearful, *superstitious* Diana-worshippers became firm believers who trusted their souls to the God unseen by human eyes.

(e) An *ungrateful* runaway thief became a willing and devoted servant of the Lord, ready to hand himself back to his former master.

Ask how these great and unusual changes of character came about. What did all these people have in common?

Closing theme. Remind the children, whichever line of revision you have followed, that wherever Paul went, his one great aim was to preach *Jesus Christ, and Him crucified (1 Corinthians 2.2)*. This was the message (though often despised and dismissed) which changed the course of history, which transformed the lives of so many we have learned about, and which alone can convert children – *to open their eyes so that they may turn from darkness to light and from the dominion of Satan to God, in order that they may receive forgiveness of sins.* (Paul's word to King Agrippa.)

Series 5
Genesis (Part II)
GOD'S GREAT PLANS

26 – God Begins a Plan with Abraham

What does the Bible mean by faith? How do we please God? How can we become Christians? As we learn how the Lord called Abraham, these questions can be answered in a real and practical way.

27 – God Tests Abraham and Reveals His Plan

What a hard thing God asked Abraham to do! What would happen if the Lord tested our love? But Abraham's obedience enabled him to share a part of God's great plan. We too must realise what it cost the Lord to give His only Son for us.

28 – Lot Experiments with His Own Plan

Abraham put the Lord first. Lot 'chose for himself'. Which plan turned out more successfully in the end? Which course will we follow?

29 – God's Plan for Finding Isaac's Wife

What wonderful and amazing things the Lord does for those who love Him. This was an unusual way to find a wife, but she was the right person, in the right place, at the right time. Have we ever experienced God's perfect guidance in our lives?

30 – Esau Sells His Share in God's Plan

Esau sold his princely position for a bowl of soup. Do we

treat our Gospel opportunities just as lightly?

31 – God's Plan of Grace

Everyone can see that Jacob did not deserve God's kindness. Nor do we. Yet he was shown that wonderful ladder and heard God's great promises. Have we been shown the way to make contact with God?

32 – Jacob Becomes Israel

First, God spoke to Jacob. Now Jacob wrestles with God. The Lord always takes the initiative but have we ever struggled in our search to know and find Him?

33 – Joseph is Shown God's Plan in His Dreams

How the Lord loves to share His ways with those who are young! How important it is for us to seek Him early so that we may find Him. He will teach us His ways and train us for His service, like Joseph.

34 – The Plan Unfolds – Strangely at First

From favourite son down to the slave market. Up from slave to head of a nobleman's household. Then down into prison again, and up to supervisor. What enabled Joseph to remain calm and victorious in these traumatic circumstances? Can *we* say that the Lord is with *us*?

35 – The Dreams Come True

The brothers have a guilty conscience and are even more frightened when they discover that Egypt's Prime Minister is Joseph. How will we feel when we find ourselves standing before the Judge of all the earth?

36 – The First Plan Completed

Now Joseph sees it all. He was sent to Egypt by the Lord to prepare for the famine. Instead of facing disaster and death, Israel's family can move to the land of plenty. The Lord God saw the danger we were in, and long before we were born He planned to send His Son to save us from the punishment of sin.

37 – Revision

An opportunity to look back through the pages of this royal family's history. The Saviour promised to Abraham, Isaac and Jacob has now come. And we, who were once

outside that family can become children of Abraham if we
put our faith and trust in the Saviour, as he did.

God Begins a Plan with Abraham (26)
The Call of Abraham

Genesis 11.27-12.9; 15.1-7; 17.1-27; Hebrews 11.8-16

Aim: To show from the life of Abraham what real faith is. To
teach the children how to respond to the Lord's call.

Teachers' Introduction

This lesson teems with Gospel applications. Teachers
should make an effort to have pictures of ancient Ur available. (Several Bible dictionaries and Old Testament history
texts include such pictures.) We shall pick out six aspects of
faith which cry out for attention from this narrative. Younger
classes may not be able to deal with them all – and certainly
it is more important to teach faith than the history of
Abraham. But remember that the children are less likely to
receive the spiritual lessons if the rest of the lesson lacks
interest and excitement.

Lesson Outline

Draw a vivid picture of Abraham and his way of life in Ur
and later in Haran. Although he lived 4,000 years ago, in
many ways life was not so different from ours. Ur was a
sophisticated, riverside city. There were busy streets, civic
buildings, libraries, schools and a bank. The secret of glass
making was known to the people of Ur. The town jeweller
made exquisite necklaces and ornate decorations for his
clients (show pictures).

The citizens were undoubtedly proud of their civilised
ways. The temple to the moon goddess provided a focal point
in the city, but it was the temple of an evil, false religion
which promoted and even made money from immorality.

Compare Ur with our modern, godless society. Show how
we place ourselves above any fear of the Lord. Politicians
and other leaders generally avoid any mention of God – or
even of His moral standards. The people of 2000 BC and

2000 AD are very similar in this way.

(1) **Faith – the fear of the Lord.** Abraham feared and respected the Lord. He believed that he and his fellow men had offended and sinned against the Judge of all the earth. It was this godly fear which caused Abraham to respond to God's call and to follow the Lord Who would show him a better life and an eternal home – *the city which has foundations, whose architect and builder is God (Hebrews 11.10).*

The first lesson which we learn from Abraham's faith is that we too must become 'afraid'. We must realise that we are also living in a City of Destruction, and that one day God will judge all people for their wilful and arrogant rebellion. We must wake up and realise how short-lived are the pleasures and boasts of this world – that nothing here is sure and reliable. We must not just say we believe in God, we must ask Him to so work in our hearts that we begin to feel our great need to be saved from our sin.

(2) **Faith – not good works but obedient trust.** When the Lord called Abraham, how did he respond? He did not try to justify himself or reform his life, trying to prove to God that he could earn his own way to Heaven. Abraham showed no confidence in himself. He simply listened to God and obeyed His instructions.

Many proud people have refused to admit their failure and tried to earn a place in Heaven for themselves. But the Bible tells us this is a disastrous policy. Instead it urges us to admit our sin and put our trust wholly in the Lord Jesus Whose death at Calvary is our only hope.

(3) **Faith – separation from the world.** God called Abraham to leave Ur and Haran, his family, his friends and his way of life, and step out into an unknown world. Now came the test – would Abraham really be prepared to do this? Would his belief in God stretch to this practical and difficult decision?

Soon the 'for sale' notice was up outside his door and he was busy buying all the equipment needed for a long journey and an outdoor life. Soon he bade his friends and relatives farewell and began this 'strange' adventure with the Lord.

In practical terms what does becoming a Christian mean to

us? Like Abraham we must be prepared to cut our ties with this world. We must be different from our unbelieving friends and set our hearts and minds on eternal things.

We may have to make a break with some of our old friends and pastimes. We shall change our reading habits, be much more careful what we watch on television, and face the scorn and annoyance of our friends when we are no longer interested in their parties and discos. Jesus said we cannot serve God *and* serve the world. All Christians must be like Abraham – willing to leave the world and follow the Lord.

(4) Faith – is receiving God's promises. We can imagine that soon after Abraham moved off with his camels and horses, with Lot (his nephew) and with the few possessions they could take with them, the neighbours gathered round to gossip about his mad decision. Why should an elderly man who had acquired a nice home, a successful business and a place of respect in the community, want to throw all these assets to the wind? And all for nothing! Perhaps they did not like to tell Abraham to his face, but they probably all agreed that he was a fool. But so busy were they enjoying their noisy pleasures, they had not heard the wonderful promises made by God to Abraham. Briefly list these to the class.

(a) God was going to give Abraham a land for the eternal possession of himself and his family.

(b) God was going to make a great nation from Abraham, bless his friends and protect him from his enemies.

(c) Even more wonderful – God's great plan to save men and women of every nation and every generation would be fulfilled through a member of Abraham's family – the coming Saviour.

Show the class how pathetic this world's goods look compared with the 'solid joys and lasting treasure' of the Lord's people. Name some of these to your class – the relief of sin forgiven, the joy of knowing the Lord personally, the comfort of His presence, the sure guidance of His Word, the hope of Heaven, the privilege of representing Him, King of kings and Lord of lords, in this world. It is like asking a child to choose between chocolate and boiled cabbage – there is no comparison!

(5) Faith – believing God can do the impossible. Tell

how the Lord led Abraham and his company into a beautiful land full of potential for the future. Though Abraham himself was always a nomad (in later years he had to buy the land to bury his wife), yet God firmly promised that the whole land would one day belong to his family. Comment on how the Lord protected him from his enemies, and even from the results of his moments of failure and sin.

Use an illustration of trust appropriate for the age of your class, eg: at first a little child eyes the sea or swimming pool with fear and nervousness. But once the child has exercised some trust, and gone into the water, he gradually realises that far from hurting him, it will support him and give him fun and pleasure. As a result his trust quickly grows.

Show how faith should grow like this. At first Abraham was nervous and inclined to lingering doubts, but as the Lord proved to be so reliable a Friend and Guide, Abraham found it less and less difficult to trust Him implicitly. So it was, when the Lord promised Abraham that Sarah would have a son, even though both were now far too old to expect a child, Abraham believed God and this pleased the Lord more than anything else. Remind the class that God wants to do impossible things for us too. He wants to turn sinful children into 'saints'. He wants to give frail mortals eternal life. He wants to change fallen, corrupt hearts into hearts full of love and kindness. But we must trust Him to do so.

(6) **Faith – a gift of God.** The Bible tells us that faith is a gift of God, and the Lord Jesus said, *Ask, and it shall be given to you (Matthew 7.7).* The Lord understands if at first our belief is almost overwhelmed by unbelief *(Mark 9.24).* But if we ask Him to help our unbelief, He will, and our first small steps of faith will grow into a sure and certain trust.

Visual Aid

A handmade map simply showing Ur, Haran and Canaan will add interest to this lesson. It could be 'decorated' with a tent such as Abraham lived in.

God Tests Abraham
and Reveals His Plan (27)
The Offering of Isaac

Genesis 22.1-19; Hebrews 11.17-19

Aim: Just as the Lord taught Abraham the way of salvation, so our aim will be to teach the same to our class.

Lesson Outline

Help the class to imagine the joy which the baby Isaac brought to his parents, who were old enough to be his great-grandparents! Imagine their delight when he took his first steps around their tent, and as he said his first words. Imagine their pride as the growing boy mastered the skills of an Eastern shepherd. Even greater must have been their joy as young Isaac uttered his first prayer and put his trust in the Lord their God.

Most children have experienced special attention from elderly relatives and will appreciate just how much love Sarah and Abraham must have felt towards the child of their old age who embodied so many of God's promises to them. Then surprise the class by recounting God's strange request to Abraham (v 2). Offer Isaac as a sacrifice! What did this mean to Abraham?.

It tested his trust in God to the uttermost. The class will appreciate that any father would find it impossible to sacrifice his child, but this treasured son of his old age – how doubly impossible for Abraham! Yet Abraham had known and trusted and loved the Lord for many years. He knew that the Lord's commands are perfect, and everything God said could be completely trusted.

As Abraham pondered God's request he must have realised that sacrificing Isaac would mean sacrificing all God's other promises. Without Isaac there could be no great nation, no promised land to be inherited, no descendant in Whom the world could be blessed.

Yet God had given His word to Abraham on all these matters and insisted that each would be fulfilled through

Isaac. Then Abraham thought of something – 'Perhaps God will raise Isaac from the dead? This must surely be the solution to this hard problem.' Abraham was sure of it.

God had definitely said that He would give Abraham descendants (grandchildren and great-grandchildren and so on) through Isaac. Therefore Abraham became convinced that God would raise Isaac up again. This is confirmed in *Hebrews 11.19*, which the teacher should 'flag up' in the Bible for easy location, and read. So Abraham knew he must trust God and obey His commands.

Remind the class that God's command to us is to surrender our selfish ambitions and 'idols' and seek Him with all our hearts. His Word teaches us about Calvary, and how the Saviour died to take away the punishment of sin on behalf of all who turn to Him for forgiveness. Here our trust is put to the test. Will we give up our 'idols' and trust in the Lord Jesus to save us and change our lives? Sometimes it is easier for young people to make grand-sounding promises like, 'I promise to give my life to God,' than to be willing at the present moment to give up their next Sunday football game – or its equivalent – for Him.

An extraordinary double lesson for Abraham: relate the events which took place on Mount Moriah:–

(a) How Abraham and Isaac arrived there with the tools of sacrifice, but no sacrificial animal. (b) Abraham's faithful reply to Isaac's question. (c) The agonising moment as Abraham lifted the knife to kill his own dear son. (d) The absence of any reference to a struggle by Isaac, who was quite grown up (so that he carried all the wood up the mountain), suggesting that he was a willing and trusting partner in this venture. (e) God's intervention, when He said, 'Now I know . . . ' (Of course God already knew, but it was necessary for Abraham to express his trust in God.) (f) God's provision of the ram.

God shares a 'secret'. Explain that Abraham named this hilltop – 'The Lord will Provide'. What would God provide? Was Abraham only thinking of the ram who had died in Isaac's place? No, he was thinking also of the great sacrifice for sin which must be made one day. Ask the class Whom the Lord God provided as a sacrifice for our sins near this very spot, many years later.

Then draw their attention back to *Genesis 22.12* and the touching words, *Now I know that you fear God, since you have not withheld your son, your only son, from Me.* Quote *John 3.16* (and possibly also *1 John 4.9-10*) telling how God so loved the world that He sent and gave His only begotten Son – the Lord Jesus Christ – so that we might be saved.

Feeling sorrow. Explain how, 2,000 years before Jesus was born, Abraham experienced what it meant to give up willingly his treasured, only son, and from this he learned and *felt* a little of what it would cost God the Father to give His only Son for us. The Saviour went through the humiliation of a shameful cross so that He might bear in His body the sins of all His people *(Acts 2.23, 1 Peter 2.24)*. By this experience Abraham could grasp how much God loved sinful people, and the lengths to which He was ready to go to make their salvation possible.

Does such a God deserve to be criticised and blasphemed by the men and women whom He is willing to save at such cost to Himself? Ask any members of the class who have already sought and found the Lord how much they owe their Saviour. (Turn them to hymns such as Frances Havergal's *Thy life was given for me.*)

Feeling joy. The Lord Jesus Christ said (2,000 years after Abraham), *Abraham rejoiced to see My day, and he saw it and was glad (John 8.56).* Abraham realised that God would provide a Saviour for his sin, Isaac's sin and the sin of all those who belong to the family of faith. That is why he named that place – Moriah – *In the mount of the Lord it will be provided,* or seen (v 14). No wonder he was glad.

Ask the children if they ever realised that far from being a distant, tragic figure in bygone history, Jesus was God's Son dying in the place of each of His people, bearing every one of their sins and therefore able to save them to the uttermost.

Visual Aid

Make three cards with the words ABRAHAM, ISAAC and GOD'S PROMISES. Place the cards in order on a background sheet and draw an arrow from ABRAHAM to ISAAC, and from ISAAC to GOD'S PROMISES. Put a question mark underneath the card marked ISAAC. During the course of the lesson remove this card to show the question mark. This will help the class to see Abraham's great dilemma.

Lot Experiments with His Own Plan (28)
Abraham and Lot Part Company

Genesis 12.4; 13.5-13; 14.10-16; 18.16-33; 19.1-30, especially 19.1, 15, 17 & 26; also 2 Peter 2.6-8

Aim: To illustrate from the life of Lot the disastrous policy of compromise. To urge the class to give themselves whole-heartedly to the Lord.

Lesson Outline

Challenge the class by describing the policy of many children. They come to Sunday School, they hear God's wonderful Gospel, they would like to be Christians and go to Heaven. But at the same time they have certain ambitions and pleasures in this world (mention examples appropriate to your class). The choice is a hard one, until Satan begins to whisper an alternative which seems to be an ideal solution to the problem. 'Why not do both at once?' he suggests. 'Continue going to Sunday School, read your Bible, pray to the Lord. But what harm would there be in keeping the old pleasures too?'

Is this a good policy? Has it worked in the past? Does God bless it? Today's lesson will give us the answers to these questions.

Lot's background. Describe how Lot knew the Lord. Having come from Haran with his uncle Abraham he had lived with him for many years. He had shared the benefits of being a member of a family which served God. He had seen how God had guided Abraham to this new land and had watched their flocks multiply.

Day-dreams. Yet Lot began to be dissatisfied. Like a teenager who becomes discontented with home, he began to look around. He began to take an interest in the things which unbelieving people set their sights on. He wished he could have their pleasures from time to time.

Take a large sheet of paper and fold it in three, so that the two outside pieces meet in the middle. On the inside draw the picture of Lot's choice as seen opposite.

LOT'S CHOICE

EITHER   OR

The Barren mountains of Canaan.   The rich fertile plain of Jordan near to the evil city of Sodom.

Fold the picture in as shown and on the flaps print these words.

Unfold as lesson proceeds.

VA 7 – Visual Aid for use with Lesson 28 – 'Lot Experiments with His Own Plan.

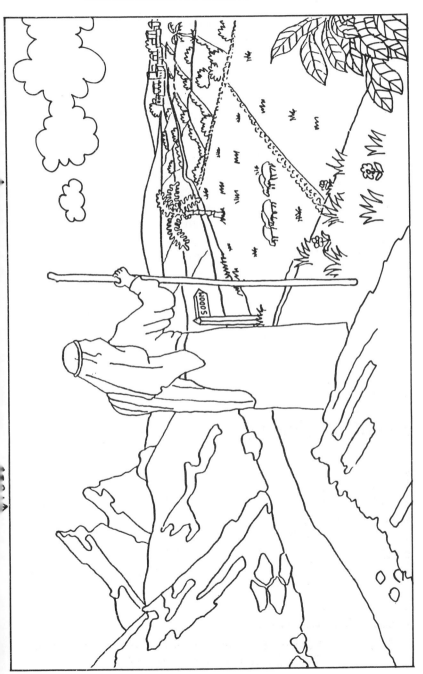

He began to day-dream with plans of his own. He had been to Egypt with his uncle and seen how sin and sorrow are the price to be paid for a worldly, self-seeking life. While Lot did not want to become an unbeliever, he nevertheless began to wish he could become successful, influential and rich in a big city. He wanted to be seen and admired wearing rich clothing and possessing luxuries. Soon he began to think of Abraham as narrow-minded and old-fashioned.

An opportunity. One day when Abraham and Lot's men quarrelled, Abraham suggested that the two families should separate and farm different parts of the land. Instead of telling his nephew where to go, Abraham offered Lot the right to choose. There was the lonely, mountainous region to the west or the rich, fertile plain of the Jordan to the east.

How did Lot choose? Did he pray to the Lord and ask His guidance in this important matter? Did he consider his uncle? The Bible tells us that *Lot chose for himself (Genesis 13.11).* He thought only of how his flocks and crops would increase down in the richer pastures of the Jordan. He thought of how he could trade in the well-populated city of Sodom.

However, because he realised Sodom was such an evil place he did not want to live *inside* the city. So he moved his home nearby, imagining that he could get some of the 'benefits' without actually being part of it. Perhaps he even justified his decision by claiming to influence Sodom for good.

Jesus spoke of the two roads of life, the wide and the narrow roads. He taught His listeners to choose *between* these roads. He mentioned no middle road – no path of compromise.

A success story? At first all seemed to go well for Lot. While Abraham followed the same routine up on the mountainside, Lot's life seemed to be full of change and advancement. His wealth increased as his business grew. But we soon discover that he had moved into Sodom *(Genesis 14.12).* His business had become fully tied up with this city, and his family had developed close friends and associations. After some years Lot was even appointed as a kind of magistrate or 'mayor' of the city and was to be found sitting in the seat of public office, an open-air civic 'throne' constructed near to the auspicious main city entrance *(Genesis 19.1)*. His ambitious ideas seemed to have paid off.

Was this true? How did God view Lot's career? What was the real truth about it? Did his 'success' last? *Genesis* gives us the answers.

(1) Lot soon lost all his wealth and possessions. The sin of Sodom had become so great and grievous in God's eyes that He determined to judge that city. He rescued Lot and some of his family, but all Lot's prized possessions were buried under the Dead Sea together with the rest of that wicked city.

(2) God had promised Abraham that He would not destroy Sodom if there were even ten righteous people there. Yet He could not find even ten. What does this tell us about Lot's influence for good in the city while he was a magistrate or mayor? It was in fact a complete failure.

(3) Lot's own family had come to love Sodom more than God *(Genesis 19.26 and 30-36)*. Far from Lot influencing Sodom, the reverse was the case. Even after Abraham had rescued Lot from a foreign invader Lot did not take the opportunity to resettle elsewhere. And even if he had wanted to leave, he could no longer do so. Money-making, possessions, the love of power and prominence, etc, all held him in their grip and Lot could not break their spell. Also, his family had become intoxicated by the wicked city and refused to go.

(4) Finally, the New Testament tells us that Lot lost his peace of mind *(2 Peter 2.8)* – he *felt his righteous soul tormented*. Knowing what was right, Lot could not really find peace of soul in such a place. His conscience troubled him. The price he had to pay for his popularity was high. The people of Sodom did not really want a man who would not drink and swear, who refused to take bribes and who tried to keep his family pure. Lot paid dearly to satisfy their demands, and although he longed for some real friendship and help, he had to avoid Abraham, whom he was too ashamed and embarrassed to meet.

Rescued by the Lord. When the angel of the Lord led Lot reluctantly out of Sodom on the day of its destruction, Lot was a destitute, bankrupt man. Had it not been for the kindness of the Lord and the intercession of his uncle, Lot's body and soul would have both been lost in the destruction of that wicked city.

Our choice. Suggest to the class that it is hard to realise that Lot lived four thousand years ago. His story might have appeared in any of our newspapers today. Certainly many Sunday School teachers could tell of children who used to be regular and enthusiastic members of their classes but who tried to lead a spiritual 'double life'. At first such children or young people were certain and sincere in their claim that a few worldly interests would make no difference to their attendance at Sunday School and their willingness to please the Lord. But gradually they kept away from the church. They discovered the truth of the Lord Jesus' words, *No one can serve two masters (Matthew 6.24).* They came to love the world, not the Lord. Sadly many of these people discover that the world is a cruel master, unlike the Lord.

Cruel disappointment. Soon the excitement and novelty of its goods wears off and many find they cannot cope without the help of cigarettes, drink, loud music or some other drug for the mind. Secretly they are miserable and sometimes wish they could return to the Lord, but Satan has wound his web around them and, without asking the Lord for help, they are no longer able or free to escape. Finally old age and death arrive and Satan snatches away the few hard-earned pleasures and possessions which once alleviated the misery.

Warn your class not to be fooled by Satan's promises or the 'success' stories they read and hear, which tell only half the story. Urge them to give themselves utterly and completely to the Lord Who has riches and treasures beyond description in store for all who love Him. If there is time, summarise some of the mighty blessings of conversion to Christ.

Visual Aid

Use the visual aid illustrated on pages 130-131 (VA 7) to help the class see the choice which Lot had to make.

God's Plan for Finding Isaac's Wife (29)
Isaac and Rebekah

Genesis 24; Ephesians 3.17-20

Aim: To relate this example of the Lord's lovingkindness to His servants in such a way that the children may realise the extent to which He is willing to help, save and bless them.

Lesson Outline

Show the class (particularly younger classes) a bottle of sand and a picture or map of the night sky. Remind them that following Abraham's act of obedient willingness to offer Isaac, the Lord promised Abraham that his family would one day become as difficult to count as the sand on the sea-shore or the stars in the sky *(Genesis 22.17)*. What a promise to an elderly man with one son!

God had also promised Abraham that He would give his family the land of Canaan as far as he could see to the east, the west, the north and the south. Yet at the time when Sarah died he had to buy the ground to bury her. Soon we shall see how God's plans began to come true and how His promises to Abraham were all fulfilled. And let us remember that Abraham believed God's words long before many of them came true. How much more, therefore, we should believe, because we have seen so many of God's promises fulfilled already.

An important matter. With this background, explain the importance of finding a wife for Isaac. How would most people have approached this matter? A rich, yet unsettled man like Abraham might have taken the opportunity to arrange a diplomatic marriage for his son (as kings and queens of history have done). Perhaps Isaac could have married into one of the tribes of the land to secure recognition and security for his family. But the Canaanites did not believe in the true God, so Abraham knew this would be wrong.

A rich young man like Isaac might well have looked out for a wife who appealed to him on the grounds of her beauty alone. However, both father and son were anxious to please the Lord.

It is never too early to remind children that their choice of a husband or wife will be one of the most important they will ever make – yet it is often a decision they must make while still young and inexperienced. How will they approach the subject? Will they think only of pleasing themselves? Will they judge only in terms of looks and money, or will they be guided by the values of God's Word? The Bible teaches that if we belong to the Lord we shall look to Him to guide us, and we shall want to be certain that our lifelong partner also loves and serves Him.

Instructions for Eliezer. Abraham was certain that Isaac's wife should not come from Canaan, yet he was equally certain that Isaac must not leave the Promised Land. How then could a wife be found? The answer to this dilemma was clear in Abraham's mind. The Lord, the God of Heaven, must lead them to the right wife. Eliezer must be sent to Haran, supported by prayer, to seek a wife for Isaac. [Verse 2 identifies the servant as being the oldest of Abraham's household, who was undoubtedly Eliezer *(Genesis 15.2).*]

Describe how the servant took his long camel journey to Haran. Three men were earnestly asking God's blessing and guidance in this great quest – Abraham, Isaac and the servant. Tell the class how glad the Lord is to answer earnest prayers. Sometimes He delays His answers, especially if we are only half-hearted, but on this occasion His guidance was swift and clear.

God's lovingkindness. Explain that, whereas many men might have been nervous and anxious on such a venture, Eliezer was calm and confident because he too trusted the Lord. He had served Abraham for many years and had seen firsthand how often the Lord answered prayer, intervened in their affairs, protected them and helped them. He was well used to the active guidance of God, and so he realised that God would guide in a remarkable way, just as He had done in the past.

Assure the class of the Lord's lovingkindness to them if they have trusted Him. He is the Lord Jesus Who came to suffer and die on the cross to take the punishment due to all those who are sorry for their sin. Even now He is preparing a place in Heaven for all who believe and trust Him. Of course they can trust such a Saviour to guide them!

Rebekah passes the test. Explain how Eliezer's prayer was swiftly answered when he met Rebekah. Many girls might have acted with charm and grace if confronted by a young, good-looking and wealthy suitor. But Rebekah showed the same kindness to a weary, elderly travelling servant. Though she was 'off guard' and unaware what Eliezer's mission was, she behaved as a gracious, understanding and godly person. This world judges people by outward appearance, skill in examinations, success in exhibitionism, etc, but Eliezer was able to see what Rebekah was really like.

Describe Eliezer's silent gaze as he waited to see if Rebekah would act out the secret sign agreed between the Lord and himself. Imagine his joy as Rebekah offered to water the camels also, and then disclosed that her father was none other than Abraham's relative. No wonder that he bowed low and worshipped the Lord! Explain how all Christians have reason to be amazed at the way in which the Lord so often overrules and guides in the ordering of their lives. (You may wish to give an example.)

Picture the scene that night as Eliezer sat as an honoured guest in Bethuel's house, his animals and companions having been provided with food and shelter. After listening to this trusted servant of their relative, Rebekah's father and brother agreed that it was the Lord's guidance that she should become Isaac's wife. And, as if this were not enough of the Lord's goodness, Eliezer was able to test Rebekah's own feelings in this matter. When given the opportunity by her mother and brother to delay her departure, she agreed to leave straight away. She, too, was glad and ready to obey the Lord's great plan.

A happy ending. As Eliezer journeyed home, followed by Rebekah and her retinue of maids and her nurse, he must have been a very happy man having experienced the Lord's ability to do 'exceeding abundantly' beyond all that he had asked or thought. Every step of this seemingly impossible mission had worked out like a perfect jigsaw and now only the final piece needed to be fitted into place.

The end of this tale hardly needs to be told. Describe the way in which Isaac met his wife-to-be. He was not at a party. He was not preening himself. Instead he was speaking to the Lord out in the fields. What blessings we miss when we neglect times of prayer! As Isaac looked up towards the sunset, he saw the silhouette of camels on the horizon.

The Lord's gift of a wife was soon to stand before him. And the Lord's choice was perfect. Far from being an arranged marriage devoid of happiness and affection, we are told that Isaac *loved* Rebekah (the original Hebrew word denotes great affection and includes 'being in love'). For twenty years Rebekah bore no children but Isaac's love for her remained strong, and after all those years the Lord heard their prayer and granted them twin sons, about whom we shall hear next week.

Trying to find words. Close the lesson by showing that the love and guardian care that God showed to Isaac is the same love that He shows to all who believe and trust Him. The apostle Paul impressed this on the believers at Ephesus (refer to *Ephesians 3*). Such was his desire to describe the wonder of God's love for His people that he mixes his metaphors. He speaks of *being rooted and grounded in love*, understanding its *breadth and length and height and depth*. He says it is a love which *surpasses knowledge*, and closes with that great verse 20, that God *is able to do exceeding abundantly beyond all that we ask or think*.

Tell your class that you love to teach them week by week, not only to warn them of sin and its consequences, but because it gives you the opportunity to tell them of your wonderful Saviour. He not only died to forgive all His people and set them free from Satan's power, but He guides them step by step throughout life's journey, doing amazing and wonderful things, beyond their greatest dreams. Then, after a lifetime of tender care and lovingkindness, He welcomes them to His heavenly home. How tragic to turn away from such a Saviour and Guide and to miss a lifetime of adventure with Him!

Visual Aid

Copy out the phrases quoted from *Ephesians 3.17-20*.

Show these to the class as you explain them and encourage them to learn the words by heart.

Esau Sells His Share in God's Plan (30)
Esau Despises His Birthright

Genesis 25.19-34; 26.34-35; 27.1-41; Hebrews 12.16-17

Aim: To show the children what they pass up when they despise and reject the Gospel.

Lesson Outline

Tell the story of a boy or girl who was chosen to represent their school at some special international event. Explain how every child would have given anything to go, but the choice fell on this particular boy. The Parents' Association held fêtes and jumble sales to raise the funds for the air fare, and the other children worked on making the necessary kit. The headmaster was at the airport early in the morning to see the boy off and to pass the greetings of the school to the host country.

Imagine the dismay when the lucky boy turned up too late to catch the aeroplane. His only excuse – that he had over-slept! Would anyone accept such a pathetic reason? Did an extra hour in bed mean more to him than this once-in-a-lifetime opportunity? What about everyone else's money and work which had been thrown away?

Tell the class that in this lesson we deal with a man who threw away an infinitely greater opportunity for the sake of a bowl of soup.

Tell how Isaac and Rebekah lived happily together but had no children for many years. They took their sorrow to the Lord and He answered their prayer. Rebekah prepared for the great day when she would have a child. Describe her extra discomfort before the birth and the Lord's message to her – that she would have twins, and His strange prophecy that the older would serve the younger.

Esau – his attitude to life. Help the class to picture the two boys as they grew up with their different ways (*Genesis 25.27*). Some of the differences were physical but other differences were more profound. The New Testament describes Esau as a *godless* man *(Hebrews 12.16)*. The word used by the writer literally means 'threshold walker' (including 'accessible' or 'wide open'). It was an expression which meant that Esau was a very undisciplined and 'floppy-minded' person; far too easy-going, having little respect for anything. He had no 'reserve'; no inner principle of discernment.

These days, people often admire this kind of character. Esau treated even sacred and solemn things flippantly. He was wide open to each and any influence and impulse which swept through his mind.

It is easy to imagine him when we think of the many 'Esaus' around us today. Their friends admire them, they are very popular, and good at making everyone laugh, but they could not be trusted with anything really important. When all is plain sailing they may appear to be good leaders, but when troubles arise they let everyone down. They are people who change their minds a lot; change with every fashion which comes along; have no loyalties; have no clear standards.

Esau's careless marriage. Esau knew how much the Lord meant to his parents. His grandfather Abraham had spoken to him of how God had promised to bless and protect his family in a special way, because it would be used by God in His great plan to give the Bible and then the Messiah. Esau knew that to become the head of such a family was the greatest possible privilege and responsibility. But there were rules to be kept.

The matter of his marriage partner concerned his family. Esau was their 'Prince of Wales', the eldest son and the heir to the family promises. Help the class to imagine Isaac and Rebekah discussing this problem around the evening camp fire. Like Abraham before them, they were anxious that Esau should not marry into the local Canaanite families – because they were godless and their culture full of immoral practices.

Imagine his parents' grief when Esau announced that he had married two Canaanite girls. Had he no interest in his future responsibilities? Had he no awareness of the importance of such a decision? As for God – Esau did not seem to care what He thought about it.

How can we avoid being like Esau?

(1) Guard our souls. Warn the children never to adopt or slip into Esau's flippant ways. Urge them – even those who are not converted – to respect God. Even if they do not yet know Him, they should treat His name with reverence.

Teach them that marriage and relationships should never be treated lightly. Though they may still not have found the Lord as their own personal Saviour, earnestly encourage them to keep one hour a week for Sunday School. Urge them never to leave the doorway of their souls wide open for Satan to trample in and out as he pleases, or they will become lifelong enemies of God, never able to receive His blessing and help.

(2) Value our Gospel privileges. Nearly all children have some treasure (valuable to them at least) with which they would never part. You would think that Esau's treasure would have been his birthright – his right to inherit and become head of the Lord's family. Explain how surprising it was then that he should accept Jacob's suggestion that he swap it for a bowl of red, lentil soup.

Explain the circumstances, but more importantly, convey the attitude which this arrangement demonstrated. Outwardly he might not admit it, but really Esau was telling God a lot. It was as if he were saying something like this: 'The things that really matter to me are food, fun and pleasure. I'm not bothered about inheriting a special place in God's chosen family. What I enjoy *now* is more important than some distant promise of heavenly treasure. You may have loved me and called me – but I don't particularly care. Much more important is getting something to eat. I want You out of my life – my new wives will make me happy, and this soup is marvellous.'

If properly expressed even the youngest child should see the shallowness and heartlessness of Esau's attitude. Has any boy or girl ever been hurt when something they have worked hard to make has simply been thrown away by another child, or by a teacher or parent? How much more is the Lord God 'hurt' when all His costly work to save souls is disregarded by us?

Go on to ask the children if they do not treat the Lord in a similar way to Esau. What do they throw away when they turn from the Lord? This is what they are saying in effect:– 'I know the Bible tells us that we were made in God's image to know and love Him – but I'd rather live and die like an animal. God tells me that He loves me and sent His only Son to suffer and die for people like me – but it doesn't move me. I'd rather enjoy my sins. God promises that if I belong to Him, I shall be an heir of Heaven – but I am more interested in my prospects here and now.'

(3) **Don't get proud and presume on God's blessing.** Esau got the soup. As the years went by he chose to forget the exchange with Jacob – probably he thought of it as a joke. In the back of his mind he assumed that the family inheritance must be his – after all he was his father's eldest son.

But he was wrong. Abraham and Isaac humbly received God's favours to them. They valued them very highly and never for a moment thought that they deserved them or were entitled to them. Esau was the opposite. He despised God's favour, thought nothing of it, and then when the time came for his father to die, he thought he was still entitled to it. But God had taken his attitude seriously. When Esau failed to appreciate his birthright and sold it, God took note of it. Esau had cast his vote against God's blessing.

Do we, by our behaviour and attitude, tell God we do not want His blessing? Only those who truly recognise their sin and place their trust in the Saviour will be saved.

(4) **Don't assume you can put matters right later.** Explain briefly how Jacob tricked his father and obtained the blessing. Actually it was God's will anyway that Jacob should eventually lead the family, but God did not approve Jacob's act of deception, and he received punishment as a result. But today our chief concern is with Esau. Describe his howls of anguish when he realised what he had missed. Now that it was time for him to inherit the family fortune and wear the clothes of authority and power, he badly wanted that blessing. He was filled with anger to see the earthly inheritance snatched away. *Hebrews 12.17* tells us – *For you know that*

even afterwards, when he desired to inherit the blessing, he was rejected, for he found no place for repentance, though he sought for it [ie: the blessing of inheritance] *with tears.* He wept and grieved for the material blessing, but never repented of his sin.

Too late. Remind the children that the Lord takes their attitude to Him now very seriously. Some young people hear the Gospel invitation and brush it aside. They decide to go their own way, enjoy life and leave religion until later. They reason, 'If I get cancer or grow old, I will have time to repent of my sins then, and still be sure of going to Heaven.' But the lesson of Esau is that people often become hardened and never do repent. Like him, they are driven only by a 'carnal' desire for health or material help. Esau did not want the Lord – only the blessings. We must not be the same.

Jesus taught that in hell there would be *weeping and gnashing of teeth.* Many people, like Esau, will be filled with remorse, wishing that they had not scorned and ignored the Lord in life. Let your class see how concerned you are that none of them despise their Gospel privileges and live – or die – to regret it. Urge them to repent now and begin to enjoy all the great blessings which the Lord waits to bestow.

Visual Aid

At this point in this series of lessons, teachers can introduce a family tree, listing Abraham, Isaac, Jacob and Esau, and adding other members of the family that feature in the lessons. As the series proceeds the children will remember the names and feel better acquainted with this great family.

God's Plan of Grace (31)
Jacob Is Shown a Ladder up to Heaven

Genesis 27.41 – 28.5; 28.10-22; Hosea 12.4-6

Aim: To teach 'the way back to God from the dark paths of sin'.

Lesson Outline

Remind the class that sooner or later, sin always has its bitter consequences. Rebekah probably congratulated herself on her cunning scheme to win the family blessing for her favourite son, Jacob. It had all gone according to her plan.

But Rebekah's triumph was short-lived. Soon her joy was ended when it was reported to her that Esau was filled with murderous fury and planned to kill Jacob. Rebekah frantically arranged Jacob's escape, sending him to her brother Laban, miles away in the land where she had grown up.

She hoped that they would only be parted for a short time, but in fact she never saw her beloved Jacob again. Her act of deception had cost her dearly, and it was all so unnecessary because the Lord had promised that Jacob would be made family leader anyway, in due course. If only Rebekah had trusted and waited for the Lord to act!

Briefly remind the class that whenever we turn away from the Lord and His guidance, the consequences are bitter.

Jacob's part. So Jacob, the home-loving twin, found himself leaving home under the most unhappy circumstances. His brother hated him and was threatening to kill him; his mother was broken-hearted to be parted from her favourite son; and his father shocked and deeply disappointed that his own son could take advantage of his blindness to brazenly lie and deceive him.

Jacob knew he had no excuse. He had been brought up in a family which had known and experienced the Lord God and His ways. Yet he had let ambition and greed rule him, so that instead of refusing his mother's suggestion, which he knew was wrong, he had complied.

Help the children to picture Jacob, lying down that night, in a barren place, sad and lonely. Gone were the comforts of home, the familiar voices, the sense of well-being and security. Jacob was cold and frightened, and his conscience hurt. The only pillow he could find turned out to be a stone!

But it was on this never-to-be-forgotten night, in these sorry circumstances, that the Lord met with Jacob and showed him the way to Heaven. Point out that the Lord often has to act like this. When we are surrounded by the excitement and bustle of everyday life and the company of our friends and family, when all seems to be going well and we can lift up our heads with pride, then we seldom take time to think of the Lord, and we cannot hear Him speaking above the din. But when we are miserable, ashamed of ourselves and disappointed, then the Lord in His kindness sometimes comes to reveal Himself. 'When other helpers fail and comforts flee' may we learn to seek the Friend of sinners.

What did God show Jacob? Tell the children about this amazing dream. Jacob, who was alone, cut-off from his friends, and on the run from his brother, was shown a beautiful staircase or ladder which led to Heaven. Angels were going up and down with messages and encouragements between God and people, between Heaven and earth.

Finally, God Himself spoke to Jacob from above the ladder. How awed Jacob was to hear the God of his grandfather Abraham and his father Isaac, speaking to him and passing down the great family blessings! How overcome he was to hear the Lord promising to go with him and keep him wherever he went, and to bring him safely back to this promised land!

What does God promise us? The children may acknowledge that God gave Jacob a dream, but they may not be able to think what this may have to do with them. God does not give such direct visions or dreams today. But invite the class to think of the words of the hymn:

> *As to the exiled patriarch*
> *That wondrous dream was given,*
> *So seems my Saviour's Cross to me*
> *A ladder up to Heaven.*

We do not need such a dream, because the Person Whom that dream depicted has since come to this world, and we have all the information about Him in the Gospels. The Lord Jesus Christ has since come down from Heaven to die on the cross and bear away sin, so that we might be forgiven and enabled to go to Heaven. God's messengers (those who wrote the Bible for us, and those who explain it to us Sunday by Sunday) give us the information we need about God's love and mercy and the way of salvation.

Like Jacob, when we are detached from this world with all its noise, and find ourselves alone with our thoughts, then we

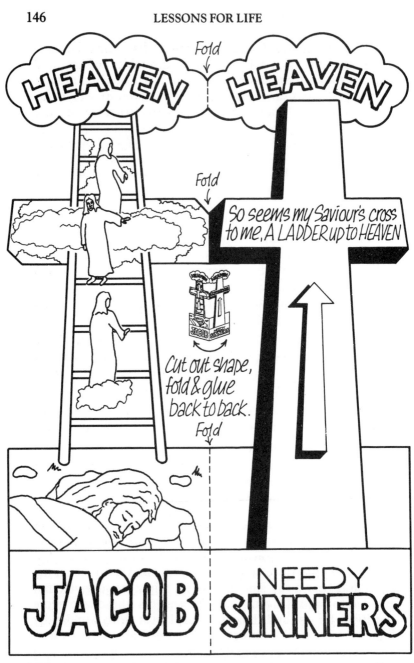

VA 8 – Visual Aid for use with Lesson 31 – 'God's Plan of Grace'.

too can appreciate God's message which tells us that there is a ladder to Heaven – a way to know God, to pray to Him, and receive His help and blessing.

The ladder or staircase which Jacob saw stands for Christ. (Older classes – read *John 1.51* to establish that Christ explains this Himself.) Jacob had never seen any other connection between earth and Heaven. The tallest tower cannot span even a minute fraction of that vast distance. Spacecraft cannot reach beyond the material universe. In other words, this dream reminds us that there is only one way by which we can be put in touch with Heaven and with God.

Not – (1) by our efforts at good lives; (2) by doing some penance; (3) by getting forgiveness from a man, such as a priest; (4) by offering up some kind of sacrifice; (5) by giving away money to charity (however good that may be); (6) by becoming a monk or nun; (7) by taking up a religion which does not believe in Christ.

There is only one ladder or staircase – the Lord Jesus Christ. Why? Because He alone has paid the price for sin. He told His disciples, *I am the way . . . no one comes to the Father, but through Me (John 14.6)*.

Jacob's response. Describe Jacob's reaction when he awoke. He was filled with a mixture of fear and gratitude. He realised that this was a very solemn place, that what he had heard and seen that night he must never forget. Do we take the Gospel message seriously?

Are we amazed that the God of Heaven and earth should speak to us, show us the way to Himself and promise to bless us? Jacob not only acknowledged that God had spoken to him, but he acted upon it. He promised that if God kept His Word, as He would surely do, then he (Jacob) would worship and serve Him. People who have met with God, who are true Christians, do the same. They do not merely believe in God theoretically; they let Him be the God of their lives. They worship and love Him and they serve Him in every possible way.

Has God ever spoken to you? If so, you will never forget it. If not, then remember Jacob and the ladder. Leave behind your pride and go to Calvary's cross and listen to the

Lord as He shows you the way to Heaven.

Visual Aid

The suggested visual aid (VA 8, page 146) will help the children understand the lesson of Jacob's dream.

Jacob Becomes Israel (32)
The Reunion with Esau

Genesis 32 – 33

Aim: To show the children that they must really be in earnest if they are to find and follow the Lord.

Lesson Outline

Take the children on a 'flashback' to last week's lesson when they saw the lonely, castaway Jacob with only his staff to call his own, sleeping on a stone for a pillow.

The journey home. Now bring them up to date as Jacob reaches Penuel. After a long journey from across the Euphrates river, he has nearly reached home, and is only forty or fifty miles away from Bethel. Once he has crossed the ford of the River Jabbok, he will be back in home territory.

But what a change! Twenty years have passed and instead of being a lonely figure, Jacob is surrounded by a vast camp. Were it a permanent site, his company would make up quite a village. Briefly describe how, through many ups and downs, the Lord had blessed Jacob, so that on his return he had a great family and a retinue of servants. In addition, he had flocks and herds of goats, sheep, camels, cows and donkeys. He possessed thousands of these animals, making him a very rich man.

Fears return. But wealth does not remove all problems, for as Jacob prepared to move his camp across the stream, he began to wonder how Esau would react to his home-coming. It was twenty years since he last saw his brother and made that lonely journey. Had Esau forgotten his rage? Had he forgiven Jacob? Or was his anger smouldering, and ready to burst out again when he heard of Jacob's approach?

Some frightening news. Tell how Jacob sent servants to

Esau. They were to greet him with respect and to gently explain that Jacob was now comfortably off, and not in need of any help. No doubt they also spoke of the generous gift which Jacob would make to Esau.

Imagine Jacob's alarm as he learned that Esau was already coming towards him and that he had with him four hundred armed men! Scenes from the past flooded back into his mind and he began to prepare for the worst.

Panic measures. First he divided his company into two sections, thinking that if one were attacked, then the other might escape. Next he turned to the Lord and prayed for His help. He admitted his unworthiness and reminded God of His past promises to make him a great nation. But still he was filled with fear, and so the following morning he took further panic measures. Several droves (herds) of animals were prepared as a gift for Esau, and these were sent on ahead – each drove being kept separate, and with a large gap between each one. Jacob evidently hoped to appease his brother by instalment after instalment of his valuable gift. (Children will be familiar with the concept of trying to placate an angry parent with various kinds of gifts!) Later that night Jacob also took his family across the ford so that he was left alone, hiding as it were behind the whole company.

A wrestling match. This turned out to be one of those never-to-be-forgotten nights, for once again God was going to come and meet with Jacob. Remind the class of how they feel as they lie in bed on the eve of a frightening experience. Perhaps the first day at a new school lies ahead of them and they are very nervous. Jacob had even more to fear, and sleep seemed far from him.

Describe how Jacob found himself, as he prayed, suddenly engaged in a mysterious and great struggle. It was dark, and he could not see, but he somehow knew that as he prayed, an angel wrestled with him, seemingly resisting him. For hours, until the dawn, the struggle went on. (*Genesis 32.30* and *Hosea 12.4-5* identify the angel as God, and *John 1.18* tells us that no man has ever seen the Father, but when God is revealed, it is by the Son. Jacob therefore was met by the pre-incarnate Son of God.)

At any time the 'Angel' could have won the battle, but it

seemed as though His purpose was to make Jacob battle and prevail! With a single touch (showing His power) He dislocated Jacob's thigh, but still allowed Jacob to get the upper hand.

I will not let you go, unless – As the sun began to rise, the 'Angel' asked to be released from Jacob's tight hold, but Jacob refused, hanging on with all his might, and pleading with his heavenly opponent to bless him and give him help.

Then the 'Angel' asked Jacob his name and told him that from that time onward his name would be changed to *Israel*, which meant that he had struggled with God and men, and prevailed.

Jacob then asked the 'Angel' for His name, but the 'Angel' simply said, 'Why do you ask?' Jacob did not really need to ask – he had realised that God was wrestling with him to make him truly *mean* his prayers.

This experience changed Jacob completely, which is why he was given a new name. He had certainly trusted the Lord before this time, and proved Him. But now he realised more than ever the importance of seeking God with his whole heart.

The winner submits. From now on Jacob would always remember his need to depend on the Lord for blessing and wisdom – the 'Angel' had left him with a wounded hip, a constant reminder that he was incomplete and weak in himself and needed the Lord. Now he was no longer afraid of Esau for he not only believed God's promises in his head, but had laid hold on them in his *heart* and with strong *conviction*.

Our struggles. Relate to the needs of the class. Many children, especially those who attend Sunday School, believe in the Lord. They may even understand Calvary and trust the Lord as their Saviour. They have had something of a 'Bethel' experience. But as they grow older and confront the world with all its temptations and doubts, the Lord often brings them to a 'Penuel' experience too. They will find a struggle going on within – do they really believe in God? Can they gladly put their life in His hands?

They may go through a long period of 'fightings and fears within, without', before finally laying hold on the Lord and determining to put all their trust in Him. From that moment they will enjoy the assurance of knowing that He is their God Who will certainly bless them and be with them all their journey through. Urge any in this position to keep up the struggle, like Jacob, and not to relax until they are certain for themselves that they are the Lord's.

Laying hold on life. Use this incident to teach newcomers that becoming a Christian is not like joining a club. When we turn to God we do not simply sign a set of beliefs and recite a creed. We actually have to *feel* how sinful we are, experience remorse and sorrow for the way we have treated our God, and long to be forgiven and made clean.

In some cases this struggle continues for some time (see *Pilgrim's Progress*), as the Lord tests our earnestness and teaches us His ways.

Moving to the front line. What happened to Jacob? Though he had behaved like a coward and sent Esau the droves of animals, he now moved forward to the front of his family and went boldly ahead to meet Esau. As we might expect the Lord had heard Jacob's prayer and had prepared Esau. Instead of receiving a hostile reception, Jacob was welcomed with kisses and embraces.

Redeemed from all evil. Soon Jacob was home again, but later God directed him to return to Bethel, where he buried any idol gods which his family had acquired, and pledged himself to God Who first spoke to him. God, for His part, continued to bless and prosper Jacob and his family through all the trials and troubles of life. Some of these adventures we shall hear in the coming weeks. When Jacob was very old and came to bless his grandchildren down in the land of Egypt, he was able to say – *The angel who has redeemed me from all evil, bless the lads (Genesis 48.16).*

Joseph is Shown God's Plan in His Dreams (33)
Joseph's Brothers Sell Him

Genesis 37.1-35

Aim: To show the children the importance and advantages of turning to the Lord while they are young.

Teachers' Introduction

The history of Joseph stands above the most imaginative fiction in possessing all the ingredients of a great drama. It has a truly wonderful hero, an intriguing, exciting and unusual train of events, a content of human behaviour which rings true to life, and a plot which grips the hopes and fears of the reader. It is a history in which injustice gives way to an ending which satisfies and pleases all.

With such magnificent material most of our lesson will be drawn directly from the Scripture and there will be no need to add illustrations. Our only additional concern will be to relate these events so that they apply to our children.

Lesson Outline

Remind the class of how Jacob returned with his large family and herds to Canaan, the land promised by the Lord to his fathers. The narrative suggests that from an early age Joseph had come to know and trust the Lord, and the Lord had given him wisdom and maturity. When only seventeen, even though he was the youngest of the brothers (except for the 'baby' of the family, Benjamin, who was the only child to have been born in Canaan), Joseph would not go along with the evil ways of his older brothers, and informed his father about them.

Jacob gives Joseph the coat. Describe how Jacob loved Joseph more than all his children because *he was the son of his old age*, and also because of his spiritual perception, and the fact that he was Rachel's son.

This led Jacob to give Joseph the famous coat of many colours – a favour which brought the young Joseph more trouble than honour. Yet we do not hear that Joseph became either aloof or bitter. He was happy to do what was best for his father, his family and the Lord.

The dreams. It is unlikely that Joseph related his dreams in a vain or ambitious spirit. We need to stress that the powerful impression which these strange dreams made upon him, led him to relate them in detail. He was mystified and awed and he almost *had* to speak of them. But the moment he did so, his suspicious, critical and vindictive brothers immediately found fault and persecuted him. In the event,

Joseph was probably kept humble by the trouble that his dreams brought him.

We divide the remainder of the lesson into four parts each with its own application.

(1) Trials as they apply to children. Often adults make light of the trials of young people and children because they seem trivial by contrast to adult problems, but to the young they are just as perplexing. But the Lord is aware of all the trials that occur, and He knows how best to help His people.

Sometimes He has to use a hard experience, even a tragedy, to make us listen to His Word, think about the purpose of life, and see our weakness and sinfulness. Sometimes He permits great difficulties to touch the lives of children who are converted to cause them to be more prayerful, to learn to exercise faith in God's power to help, or to leave some particular sin alone. Sometimes He allows others to persecute His converted children to 'prove' them, or so that their stand will be better seen and may impress others.

Therefore we should never be crushed by criticism and unkind remarks, especially if these come because we are converted, but instead we should be like Joseph, trusting the Lord's power and goodness to His children.

(2) God's overriding plan for our lives. As you describe Joseph's dreams, help the children to picture his reaction to them. He was perplexed – how could it be that his brothers, most of them older than himself, would bow down to him, and his parents also? His brothers reacted angrily, inferring that the dreams were brazen ego-trips, but Joseph seems to have sensed that the dreams came from outside himself. Jacob too, whilst rebuking outward arrogance, seems to have felt the same. Perhaps he detected in Joseph's earnestness that the boy's dreams were similar to the dream which the Lord gave him at Bethel.

Tell your class that these dreams did come true! They must wait another week or two to discover how, but this fact confirms that the dreams were from the Lord. He knew how Joseph's life would work out and how it would end. Remind the children that God knows all about us; He knows what we will be like, what we will do and when we will die. He keeps

This visual aid is like a 'sales chart' showing the ups and downs of Joseph's life. Cut out 5 pieces of card about a foot long, or more for a larger class. Make holes where shown. Draw pictures and arrows as above. Be careful when doing the words that they are not obscured when the chart is assembled. Fit together with split pins and unfold as lessons proceed.

VA 9 – Visual Aid for use with lessons in the life of Joseph.

Draw these pictures as indicated on the previous page.

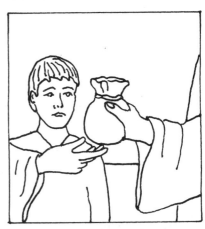

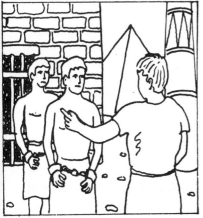

a record of all we do and think. Encourage the children to seek the Lord now and experience His forgiveness, His guidance and His blessing through life. If not, we will meet Him at death, when He will open up the record of our lives to judge us.

(3) Children used by the Lord. God knew there would be a great famine which could destroy the chosen family, and He used Joseph in His mighty scheme to save them.

The Lord loves to use young people whose hearts belong to Him. Urge the class to join the great band of children and young people like Joseph, Samuel, David and Daniel who have been greatly used by Him.

(4) Never abandoned by the Lord. Suggest that these dreams must have strangely comforted Joseph in the frightening events which were soon to come to pass in his life. Relate how Joseph's brothers took vengeance, almost killing him and then opting for a conscience-saving measure by planning to sell him to the Ishmaelites. Imagine how frightened he must have been to be hurled into a pit by his own family, and then to overhear their sinister schemes.

Hardly less frightening was the experience of being sold to total strangers and finding himself bound for Egypt to be sold as a slave in a totally foreign land. How glad he must have been to know that, even if deserted by everyone else, the Lord would be with him, and one day He would use these harrowing circumstances for some great good.

Contrast the life of unbelievers with the life of Christians. Unbelievers have no point or purpose in living, except for selfish pleasures and ambitions which are seldom satisfied. They have no heavenly Friend or Saviour to see them through the dark days. If things go wrong in their lives, they will probably stay wrong, or get even worse! The non-Christian has no security or certainty about the future. Urge the children to face these facts and follow the lonely but certain course which Joseph took.

Visual Aid

Use the 'up-and-down' chart (VA 9, pages 154-155) throughout the Joseph lessons to outline Joseph's career, and to help the children remember God's overruling care of His people. In addition, for this lesson, diagrammatic pictures of Joseph's dreams are easy to draw and add interest to the lesson.

The Plan Unfolds – Strangely at First (34)
Joseph's 'Ups and Downs' in Egypt

Genesis 39 & 40; Isaiah 55.8-9

Aim: To illustrate the sovereignty of God over the events of history and His particular care and concern for those who trust Him, through the 'ups and downs' of Joseph's life.

Lesson Outline

Give the lesson practical relevance by reminding the children that many people watching the news or reading the papers, immediately decide that there is no God ruling over the world. Explain that the whole Bible teaches us quite the opposite of this viewpoint. It asserts that – *The Lord reigns (eg: Psalms 97 & 99)*. It tells us that the God Who made the heavens and the earth overrules its events and controls its destiny. Not only does He govern history, but He especially watches over those who love and trust Him, promising to work all things together for their good *(Romans 8.28)*. What we have to remember is that we are mere mortals who are very short-sighted, and our knowledge and wisdom is very limited. Often we could hastily and foolishly misjudge God's ways.

Our lesson today will give a perfect demonstration that God's ways are not always our ways, and that His ways are far higher than ours. We learn to appreciate these great facts by following Joseph's career. Sometimes his circumstances seemed hard and cruel and yet in years to come the perfect plan and purpose of God became evident and clear to all. Urge the class to follow the reasoning (not just the exciting story) and to become much more thoughtful about these great issues of life in future.

A slave. Return to the close of last week's lesson. Let the class imagine Jacob's favourite son standing in the Egyptian market-place, being prodded and poked like an animal. Eventually someone put in a bid for him and he found himself being transported to the household of Pharaoh's captain-of-the-guard, an officer named Potiphar. Here Joseph was to do as he was told, work long hours and earn nothing but his keep.

Such a change of circumstances might have got many young men down and caused them to despair or turn to crime. But Joseph was unmoved. He knew the Lord was with him, and though perplexed, he trusted his God. Instead of sulking and skiving, he worked conscientiously, remembering that he served a Master in Heaven, not only an Egyptian officer.

Head of Potiphar's house. Soon his attitude to life was noted together with the success that followed it, and Potiphar gladly made Joseph overseer of his entire household. So completely did Potiphar trust Joseph that he left all his accounts, his banking affairs, the management of his land – everything – in the hands of this young Hebrew slave. Nor was he disappointed.

God blessed everything that Joseph did and whilst he was in charge the whole operation proved highly successful. He gained experience in managerial and commercial skills, which were to be of great importance to him in the future. But just as things were going so well for Joseph, and he had risen to great heights, suddenly he found himself plunged into disgrace and humiliation. (Be sure to emphasise this 'down' by reference to the suggested visual aid.) In one day he found himself moved from Potiphar's office into Pharaoh's jail! Why? How?

Unfair. Explain how Potiphar's wife (probably jealous at Joseph's influence in her husband's affairs) devised a spiteful scheme either to share Joseph's power or to accuse him of the very thing which he would never do. Finding herself alone in the house with Joseph, her ugly plan to seduce him came to a head. Joseph declined her advances (a) because he refused to abuse Potiphar's trust, and (b) because he refused to sin against God and do this 'great evil'. In anger she turned against him accusing him of the very sin she had suggested.

If appropriate for their class, teachers can remind children that most believers are subject to unfair and unjust treatment at school or work. The fact that they try to please the Lord and work conscientiously often gives rise to jealousy and hostility. How should they respond? Warn them against becoming priggish, or courting teacher's favour for its own sake, but encourage them to follow Joseph's example, living close to the Saviour and accepting the events of life as from Him.

Sent to prison. Describe how Joseph now had to face very unpleasant circumstances in the jail. Prisons were designed in those days to punish. Not only that, but Joseph must have wondered how long he would have to remain there. He had no family in Egypt to campaign for his release or to plead his innocence. But however distressing his conditions, Joseph knew the Lord was with him and that made all the difference. He refused to fret and despair. Instead he looked for opportunities to live and behave as all believers should and, in fact, his honesty and energy so commended him to his seniors that before long he was put in charge of the other prisoners.

Strangely enough the prison gave him many interesting experiences. Not only did he meet criminals but, because it was the prison which served Pharaoh's household, he met many high-ranking officials who had fallen from favour. No doubt they spent many hours discussing their work and their problems with Joseph – the jailer who himself was a prisoner and who showed such a very kindly concern in their affairs.

The butler and baker. Briefly explain how Pharaoh's butler and baker arrived in the prison and how Joseph was able to help them. Make a note of the fact that he did not claim any personal credit for unfolding the meaning of the dreams. He made it quite clear that God had given him the interpretation.

Help the class to feel the disappointment Joseph must have felt when the butler returned to the palace and forgot to mention his Hebrew friend. Like a child anxiously awaiting good news daily in the post, Joseph must have hoped to hear that his case was to come under review. But for two more years his hopes were dashed.

God's purpose. Point out that while everything *appeared* to be lost, the reverse was in fact the case. In the great plan and purpose of God, Joseph was receiving a complete and unique training for the high office which lay before him. Mention the following points:

(a) God was preparing his character – no longer was he the spoilt, sheltered, favourite son of an aged father. He had learned to master hard and cruel circumstances, and to turn them to account.

(b) Joseph had learned to depend on the Lord in everything he did, and the Lord, having proved his love and faithfulness in these difficult days, knew that he could be trusted with days of plenty and power.

(c) Joseph had been given practical experience and advice far beyond his contemporaries. Both in Potiphar's house and in the prison he had gained vast managerial experience, and he had mixed with men who had held the highest offices in the land. In his lonely cell he had many hours to make mental notes of all he had learned.

Gather these arguments together to show the children how wrong it is to hastily misjudge God's ways. Next week we shall be seeing how wise and perfect His ways proved to be for Joseph.

Close by reminding the class that there are two ways to look at all events. Give the following examples:–

(a) We can hear how Jesus died on the cross and think how weak and foolish God must have been to allow such a thing to happen to His Son. Or, we can listen to His Word and realise that unless the Lord Jesus had been willing personally to bear our sins at Calvary, we could never be forgiven. Far from being an act of weakness, His submitting to arrest and crucifixion was the greatest achievement of all time.

(b) We can look at the sad days in our lives, and the disappointments, and grumble at God, making them an excuse not to believe in Him. Or, we can trust Him as our Saviour and Friend Who, having given His life for us, will work all things together for our good.

(c) We can look at our world with its triumphs and tragedies and imagine it has no Creator, no Ruler, and no Judge. Or, we can allow all these events to teach us that we have a Maker to Whom this world belongs, and begin to prepare for the day when we must answer to Him.

A perfect commentary on this lesson is Cowper's great hymn,

> *God moves in a mysterious way*
> *His wonders to perform.*

Teachers should read it before the lesson and use its pictures and arguments to make these great points clear.

The Dreams Come True (35)
Prime Minister of Egypt

Genesis 41 & 42

Aim: To teach some of the great principles of grace through these moving events in the life of Joseph.

Lesson Outline

Our lesson opens with a truly dramatic turn of events. From his prison dungeon Joseph is elevated to being the second most powerful ruler in the empire of those days, all in a matter of hours, at the invitation of Pharaoh. How did this come to pass?

The butler remembers – at last! Remind the class how disappointed Joseph must have been when it became obvious that the butler had forgotten him. The two years which passed must have seemed an age, but then the butler was suddenly reminded of his dreams and recommended the Hebrew prisoner to Egypt's king.

Warning and advice. As you tell the class about Pharaoh's strange dreams and their meaning, show how Joseph went on to make very practical suggestions to Pharaoh so that people could escape the forthcoming famine. Explain that this is typical of God's grace and kindness always. When God warns of dangers to come, He also gives the way of deliverance.

Through the Bible God warns us today of the judgement which awaits us all as sinners. But at the same time we are told how Christ has borne the punishment for all who turn to Him in repentance. (How different this is from worldly advisers who can sometimes tell us what is *wrong* with things, but can never put them right!)

Power which did not corrupt. Many young men who have been given power and authority have been ruined by it. Some have been corrupted by their new-found position and have become proud, vain, self-confident, heartless, even ruthless. But Joseph's heart had been prepared by the Lord for his high office.

A dangerous position. The children will be excited to learn how Jacob's sons came to bow before Joseph as the dreams had predicted. Help the class to feel the tension of the scene. Joseph is in complete charge. Will he seize the opportunity to punish these brothers and take revenge for their treachery? Little do they realise at this moment what danger they are in.

Remind the class that men, women and children are in a similar peril. Often they do not realise that their lives are lived before the Judge of all the earth Who is already determining their eternal fate. Yet, when they should be trembling before Him, they snub Him, blaspheme His name and abuse His gifts.

Describe Joseph's wisdom in dealing with the brothers. He rules out any spite or vindictiveness. He knows the Lord has forgiven him much and he gladly forgives them. But he plans to give them the opportunity to make amends for their behaviour.

Joseph tests the brothers. Describe their horror as he accuses them of being spies. Having allowed them to soberly assess their situation in prison for three days, he finally agrees to let them go. But, he keeps Simeon hostage so that they will realise that he is in earnest when he demands that they bring Benjamin with them on their next journey.

Benjamin – Rachel's second son! The idea rang alarm in the brothers' ears. They knew how Jacob would react to losing Joseph's only true brother. Suddenly the scene of Joseph's betrayal rises before their eyes and they remember him pleading with them. What remorse they now feel for their callous indifference to his pleas. Joseph heard these laments but he did not reveal himself at this stage. Their feelings and words of repentance had first to be put to the test. What would they be prepared to do to save Benjamin?

God tests our repentance. Show the class that before

any person becomes a Christian that person must be very sensitive about his or her sinfulness. We cannot go to the Lord casually, or with a very general confession of some past sin. We must show real sorrow, not only for outward deeds, but also for the rottenness of our hearts, which lead us to act in a sinful way. Even little children can know true sorrow and remorse.

Forgiveness prepared ahead of repentance. Come next week and discover how Joseph revealed himself to his brothers – but in the meantime ask yourself if you have ever faced up to your sin and repented of it. Remember that God wants to see *genuine* shame and regret – just as Joseph did. The prayer of repentance must be meant with the whole heart, for only then will the Lord hear and forgive and bless us.

The First Plan Completed (36)
The Family Moves to Egypt

Genesis 43 – 46.27

Aim: As we bring this adventure to its happy close, we reflect on its similarities with God's plan for our salvation.

Lesson Outline

Our lesson opens with a sorrowful and elderly Jacob realising that if his family is to survive he must allow Benjamin, his favourite son, to accompany his brothers to the land of Egypt. Judah offered to stand surety for his brother and reassured his father in every possible way.

A true-to-life account. Teachers may like to pause at this stage just to point out to the children how very true to life the Bible is. What other historical literature would draw attention to such human details as those we read in chapter 43.6-7, where we see into a family skirmish? These words sound so reminiscent of any family trying to pass blame in a different situation. How familiar the argument sounds!

Similarly the children will recognise a common situation in chapter 45.24. Even after all these years away from his family, Joseph reminds his brothers not to quarrel or 'fall out' on the journey home!

A tearful problem. Describe how they arrive, apprehensive, in Egypt with double money to placate an angry ruler. But instead they find themselves treated as royal visitors. The children will readily appreciate Joseph's problem as he set eyes upon Benjamin, his 'little' brother, now a young man. First he had to hide his emotions. Then he had to wash the give-away marks from his face.

(1) Joseph tests the brothers. Provoke the interest of your class by asking why at this stage Joseph still hid his identity – even though it was hard for him to do so. Comment on his wisdom in giving the brothers an opportunity to demonstrate that they would never treat Benjamin in the same callous manner as they had treated him. Joseph had already heard how troubled their consciences were on account of their behaviour in earlier years. Now he sets up a test situation so that they can prove themselves.

(2) Judah pleads for Benjamin. The children should become thoroughly excited as they visualise Joseph's steward opening all the brothers' sacks only to find the missing silver cup in the last sack of all – Benjamin's. Joseph demanded that Benjamin become his slave. How will the brothers react? Will they desert their unfortunate brother?

This time the thought did not cross their minds. Instead, Judah appealed to Joseph in the most touching and tender way, volunteering to take Benjamin's place.

(3) The brothers are fearful. At this point, Joseph could contain himself no longer. Describe how he sent the Egyptians out of the room and revealed himself to the brothers. Describe also their reaction – their relief and joy at seeing their long-lost brother, tempered with fear and apprehension when they considered what power he had to punish them. No wonder they were *dismayed at his presence*. Can we look forward to seeing the Lord Jesus Christ one day? Will we recognise Him as our dear Saviour or will we be dismayed in the presence of the Judge of all the earth?

(4) Joseph is satisfied. Go on to describe Joseph's mercy. Instead of showing anger and demanding vengeance, or even claiming costs for all the suffering he had endured, Joseph discharged the brothers from all blame for selling him. He looked beyond their petty unkindness, and saw God's hand in all the events that had taken place. *It was not you who sent me here, but God.*

The Lord had foreseen the great famine to come and had sent Joseph ahead to preserve the life of Israel's family and many others too. As Joseph looked back over the years he could see that all his painful experiences had been worthwhile. Soon he would be reunited with his father, and the whole family could live safely and securely in the land of Egypt. He had been battered and humiliated, but now his family could report to Jacob of all his glory and power.

The Lord Jesus will rejoice. The Lord Jesus also suffered much pain and degradation for His people at Calvary, but Scripture tells us that he went through it all – *for the joy set before Him (Hebrews 12.2)*. Our Saviour has great joy when He sees young people saved from sin, death and hell. When He sees us, who richly deserve to be punished, set free because He paid the price for us, then He rejoices. Ask the children if they are amongst those who make the Lord glad because they have experienced His wonderful gift of forgiveness and conversion.

(5) **A happy ending for Joseph and Jacob.** Bring the 'story' to a close by assuring the class that Jacob, with God's blessing, was enabled to make the move down to Egypt. At Beersheba the Lord assured him that the family promise still stood, and that after many years his descendants would return to the promised land. Help the children to picture the happy reunion between Jacob and Joseph who had once thought that they would never meet again on earth. Explain that Pharaoh welcomed Joseph's family and gave them a choice part of Egypt in which to settle.

A happy ending for us? Urge the children to read this narrative in the Bible for themselves to discover all the details which show God's mighty power which – *causes all things to work together for good to those who love God (Romans 8.28)*. Urge them, as young people, to do as Joseph did and serve the Lord while they are young, so that they too will be able to look forward to that eternal Land which the Lord is preparing for His people.

Revision (37)

Aim: To review the history of Abraham's family down to Joseph in one lesson, summarising the spiritual lessons learned in a way which will challenge the children's hearts.

Teachers' Introduction

This revision lesson should be prepared with special enthusiasm, as it provides an opportunity to draw together the separate threads which together form 'God's great plan of grace' in *Genesis*.

It will help the children see and remember individual lessons in the whole context of events. Particularly in this 'family' series, the children will enjoy relating one member of the family to another. Using a map they will trace with interest the movements of this family through four generations. As they take a bird's-eye-view of this chosen family's history, they will be helped to see God's overruling hand in His scheme to send a Saviour into the world.

Lesson Outline

Base this lesson on a family chart. Test the class to see how many names they remember. Help them to see how each member is related to the others. Will they confuse Rebekah and Rachel? Why did Joseph love Benjamin more than his other brothers? In this day and age when family drama serials are so popular we can show that God chose this particular family to teach us many valuable lessons.

Although they lived at the beginning of history this family could be compared to any other family. Despite our modern gadgets and sophisticated lifestyle, we share the same basic characteristics as Abraham's family. Probably the children have recognised various people and situations in this series as typical of their own families. Sometimes they will have seen themselves portrayed. We have watched jealousy, deceit, pride, ambition, hatred and greed surfacing in the life of this family, but four thousand years later – when man is supposed to have evolved and improved – we find these same sins ruining life.

More importantly we learn that the way the Lord dealt with this family is exactly the same as the way He will deal with us. Question the class in order to remind them of some of the great Gospel truths we have learned. These simple sentences may help to pinpoint the lessons and fix them firmly in the heart and mind:–

Positively:

(a) Abraham was called by God to leave all and follow Him – and so are we.

(b) Abraham believed what God said – and so should we.

(c) Abraham learned that God would Himself provide a sacrifice for sin – and so must we.

(d) Isaac discovered that God could do more than he could have wished or dreamed – and so may we.

(e) Jacob, lonely and afraid, saw the way to Heaven – and so can we.

(f) Later, in prayer, he clung to the Lord and would not let Him go – and so should we.

(g) Joseph, sold by his family into a foreign land, discovered that all things work together for good – and so will we.

Negatively:

(a) Lot tried to do without the Lord and failed – and we shall also fail if we do the same.

(b) Esau despised God's blessing – and we are warned never to have the same attitude.

Conclude the series by reminding the class that any person, Jew or Gentile, black or white, living in ancient or modern times, who has put or who will put their trust in the Lord, believing that He alone can save and guide through this world to live in His heavenly City, is a member of Abraham's *spiritual* family.

Series 6
John's Gospel
THE 'I AM' SAYINGS
OF THE LORD JESUS

38 – The Living Water
Jesus offered the woman of Samaria *living* water. Why are people always so dissatisfied? How does the Lord Jesus quench our thirst? Here are several vital illustrations.

39 – The Bread of Life
We spend our lives working and toiling. And where does it get us? Where can we find food which will endure to eternal life?

40 – The Light of the World
The Pharisees were blind to the blessings and glories of the Lord Jesus. The blind man was made to see. Why do people still prefer darkness to light? The Lord Jesus remains this dark world's light and if we look to Him we too will have the light of life.

41 – The Good Shepherd
Sheep may distinguish between their own shepherd and a hired man. How tragic that we are so deaf to the calls of our Maker and Saviour. How readily we listen to the thieves and robbers, and stray from the Good Shepherd. Just as the Eastern shepherd risked his life for the sheep, so the Lord Jesus laid down His life to rescue us. He is still seeking His sheep.

42 – The Resurrection and the Life

What happens when we die? Is there any hope beyond the grave? The Lord Jesus raised Lazarus and He gives eternal life to all who will believe in Him.

43 – The Way, the Truth and the Life

There are so many people offering us 'heaven'. How can we know the way? Who speaks the truth? Jesus said He is the Way. How can we be sure that we will go to live in His heavenly home?

44 – The True Vine

Do we serve any useful purpose in this life? Will our Maker be satisfied with our achievements? Jesus tells His disciples that unless they live in Him they will produce nothing.

45 – The Lamb of God

Why do we need a Saviour? What is sin? Why was it necessary for the Lord Jesus to die in our place? Who will He forgive?

46 – The Son of God

These great claims were made by the Lord Jesus *that believing you may have life in His name (John 20.31)*. Has He opened your eyes, quenched your thirst, raised you from the dead, taken away your sin?

Teachers' Introduction to Series

As Sunday School teachers we stand in awe at the way in which the Saviour used timeless, everyday illustrations to communicate His power and willingness to bless. This series of lessons will fascinate the children, not only because of the situations in which the Lord Jesus made His momentous claims, but because these circumstances occur in ordinary life today.

A word of warning. In describing the basic needs of life – water, bread, light, etc – it is easy to make the applications of these lessons very repetitive. If the lessons are given scanty thought the children will soon become bored and restless listening to similar applications. This would be a great shame because the Lord intended these 'pictures' to be rich and profound. For this reason it would be wise to read the whole series through before embarking on the first lesson. The headings provided are intended to emphasise new and fresh points for each lesson and should be followed with care.

Younger classes. With very young classes, teachers should spend more time recounting the incident which led to Jesus' claim, and then limit the number of applications to one or two. For example, in the first lesson concentrate on telling the children about the woman of Samaria, explaining how weary and thirsty she was, not only for the well-water, but for the things which only the Lord Jesus could give her, like the washing away of all her sins. This will be sufficient for little children – any further applications could confuse them.

The general message of this series for the little ones is that just as our bodies cannot manage without bread, water, light, etc, so our souls cannot survive without the Saviour.

Visual Aids

(a) A circle-chart (VA 10, see page 171) which opens up week by week to show each of the Lord Jesus' titles. Every Sunday the leader or class teacher can remind the children of the titles already learned and then go on to reveal the title for that particular Sunday. By the end of the series these names will be firmly lodged in the children's minds.

(b) Where possible teachers should provide a real-life example or picture of these items. Each lesson note begins by suggesting a way of arousing the children's curiosity – by posing a riddle which they have to solve. By this means the series of lessons gains a cohesion and interest which would be missing, were the incidents to be dealt with in an uncoordinated way.

The Living Water (38)
The Woman of Samaria

John 4.1-30 and 39-42

Aim: To show that however much we have of this world's goods we are always thirsty for more. Only the Lord Jesus knows our real need and can quench this basic thirst.

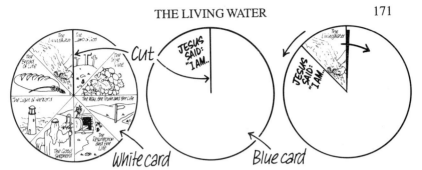

Cut two circles the same size out of card. Do lettering and drawings as shown. Cut slits. Place circles over each other. Gently slide through as lessons proceed.

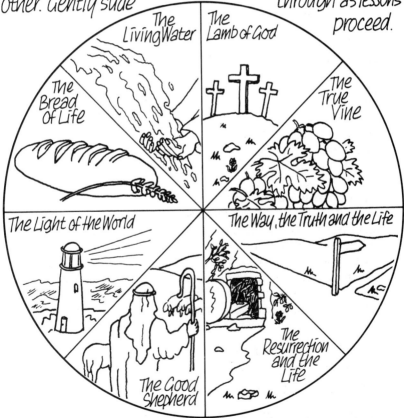

VA 10 – *Visual Aid for use with lessons on 'The "I AM" Sayings of the Lord Jesus'.*

Lesson Outline

A riddle. Teachers may like to awaken the children's interest and curiosity by asking them a riddle along these lines: what is it that we are mainly made of? We need fresh supplies of this ingredient every few hours; we get into it and put it on us regularly; we cook with it, etc, etc. What is it? (Water.)

The woman of Samaria

(a) Describe the woman whom Jesus met at the well of Sychar. Describe how she had to set off in the midday sun to fetch her family's daily requirement of water. Why was she carrying out such a heavy task at midday? Tell the children about her lifestyle, and explain how she probably had to avoid other women of the district by going to the well later than the normal time. The other women would have shunned her because of her life.

(b) To her surprise she met a Jew at the well, and soon He was asking her a favour! Explain to the class that this was unheard of, for the Jews just did not talk to Samaritans.

(c) Even more surprising, this stranger was soon telling the woman that He could give her living water, and if she drank it, she would never thirst again! What could He mean?

Water which does not satisfy. Lost at sea we might be tempted to drink water from the oceans around us, but it would make us sick immediately. The woman of Samaria had repeatedly wanted another husband, but the more husbands she had, the less happy she was. We too are always wanting something else. The world bombards us with offers of happiness (for example, on TV night after night). Even rich and powerful people have an insatiable thirst for more.

Twenty or thirty years ago it used to be said that if only people had good homes, food and clothes they would be satisfied – but now that they have fitted carpets, cars, and expensive holidays, people want more still.

We convince ourselves that what we need is new things, new sports equipment, new clothes, or new friends, but what we really need is the Lord Jesus. Without Him, we shall always be unhappy, thirsty people. Like water, we need Him every moment, every day, every year.

Water to wash. How important water is for washing. Everything in our world gets dirty – clothes, homes, cars, our own bodies. Everything needs repeated washing. The Lord Jesus knew the woman of Samaria better than she knew herself. She had sinned, and instead of seeking forgiveness she had covered one sin with another. Perhaps she had many children whose lives were a misery because of her constantly changing men-friends. Yet when this made her depressed, instead of undoing the wrong, she plunged deeper into sin. People are the same today.

The Lord knew that her sins needed washing away. She needed to be made clean. The world offers a variety of distractions to make us forget our sin. But the Lord Jesus did something to take away sin. He died on the cross so that our sins could be forgiven, and we could be made clean.

Water refreshes. The woman of Samaria, like everyone in that hot, dusty region, would always keep water for washing her feet when she got home. How refreshed she felt when she could cool her weary feet! We also use water for cooling ourselves and look forward to a pleasant dip in the swimming pool on a hot summer's day. (Older classes know how important water is for cooling sophisticated machinery, from cars to power stations.)

Often, on a hot journey, a cooling drink would give travellers in the East a new burst of energy.

The Lord knew that this woman's life needed a new, fresh start. She needed a new heart, a new beginning. If she would turn to Him and receive the living water He would give, she would be given a new start in life.

The Lord Jesus alone can bury our past and give us a 'clean sheet'. All Christians know what it is to be made 'new creatures'; new people, who, instead of hating God, find their hearts full of love towards Him and want to live to please Him.

The woman of Samaria went back to her town to tell her friends that she had found a Saviour, Someone Who had told her all she ever did, and they too went to meet Jesus and soon believed Him to be God's Son.

Water is free. One of the great things about water is that it is virtually free. We have to pay dearly for every extra unit of gas and electricity, for food and clothes, and everything else, but we can keep the tap on all day and it costs very little. We do not have to manufacture water – it comes down from above. (Any water bills we may receive, cover the cost of collecting the water into reservoirs, then filtering and distributing it.)

The Lord Jesus came down from above and all the blessings He waits to give us are free. We do not have to pay for forgiveness or for a new heart. We only have to see how much we need these and ask Him with real anxiety, and He will give us an everlasting supply without our having to pay. If we did have to pay we could never be converted to God – because we have nothing with which to pay.

We must ask. Jesus told the woman that if she had only realised Who He was, she would have asked Him for the living water. Countless people today do not realise that there is a great and merciful God Who stands nearby, and Who hears the prayer of all who repent of their sin and ask for new life. If this lesson has helped you to realise Who the Lord Jesus is, and how much you need Him, go quickly to Him and ask Him for the precious gift He is willing to bestow.

People who have received the living water can say the words of this hymn –

> *I heard the voice of Jesus say,*
> *'Behold I freely give*
> *The living water, thirsty one,*
> *Stoop down, and drink and live.'*
> *I came to Jesus, and I drank*
> *Of that life-giving stream;*
> *My thirst was quenched, my soul revived,*
> *And now I live in Him.*

The Bread of Life (39)
Feeding of the Five Thousand

John 6.1-14 and 23-58

Aim: To show that life without Christ is toil and trouble which gains us nothing, and to demonstrate how superior are the blessings of a Christian.

Teachers' Introduction

In *John 6.26* the Lord Jesus disclosed that the provision of physical bread on this great occasion was intended as a sign of His power to provide *spiritual* bread. He was saddened because the crowds who chased after Him were only interested in seeing something spectacular at a *physical*, human level. The following approach to the lesson makes the analogy simple and obvious for children. The fact that 'bread' has become a slang expression for money adds to the usefulness of this lesson.

(The feeding of the 5,000, taken as an incident, has been covered in a lesson in Mark's Gospel – see 'Jesus' Power over Need', page 28.)

Lesson Outline

A riddle. Ask the children to guess this riddle: it is solid; we eat it; we need it every day; it does not taste particularly *special*, and yet we do not get tired of it. What is it? (Bread or Food.)

The Miracle. Describe how the crowds who had seen the Lord's other miracles followed Him about. They wanted to see more. Even though their motives were shallow and selfish, Jesus had compassion on them and fed them miraculously. Five thousand people (enough to fill a small football stadium) participated in this amazing event. Ask the class to imagine the reports in the newspapers and on TV if it were to happen nowadays.

As Jesus reached a great 'high' in popularity, many people wanted Him to be their king. The next day the crowds pursued Him to the other side of the lake asking for more bread and more miracles. But Jesus refused earthly honours. Instead He began to offend many of His hearers by telling them not to labour for food which perishes, but for that which *endures to eternal life*. Later the Lord Jesus told them, *I am the bread of life*. What did He mean? What is the difference between the bread we eat every day and the bread of life?

Without bread we die! Have you seen pictures of starving children? What a tragic sight. When we see such pictures we give a sigh of relief that we are never really hungry. But did you know that when God looks at us He sees our *souls* looking just as pathetic and emaciated? The part of us that matters most of all – and which will survive our bodies – has been completely neglected. The real person inside us is starving and dying because we have lived without God year after year. We are desperately in need of heavenly food, and only the Lord Jesus can provide it.

The soul's 'food' is not, of course, eaten by mouth, like bread. It is given directly to our souls by the Lord as we 'feed' on Him. When we repent of our sin and yield to Him as Lord, He puts *spiritual life* into our souls. Then, as we live and obey Him day by day, and as we pray for His help and blessing, He adds more things to that gift of *spiritual life*. He gives us spiritual feelings: certainty that we belong to Him, understanding of His ways, and much power over our sinful tendencies. This is how the soul is fed. Just as the well-nourished body can be vigorously active, so the well-nourished soul can also be active. Once we have been given *spiritual life* we can love God, understanding about Him and praying to Him. Because the soul is now active, we can *know* and *feel* the Lord in a living and personal way. Have you received *spiritual* bread in your soul?

Nutritious food. The Lord Jesus offered *food which endures to eternal life.* When He forgives us and converts us (putting spiritual life in us) something happens which will never wear off. Once a true Christian, always a Christian. Every day we follow the Lord Jesus we find out something more wonderful about Him. He gives us His joy and peace and the more we know about Him, the more we want to know, and the more we shall know. The Christian life is the most satisfying and fulfilling in the world. Many Christians have known the Lord for fifty years and more. They never tire of Him nor want worldly things to take His place. (Describe one of the older members of your fellowship.)

What must we do? – Eat, believe. The crowds wanted to know what work they had to do to obtain the 'bread' (or meat) which Jesus could give. The answer was very simple. They were to, 'Believe in Him Whom God has sent' – the Lord Jesus.

Bread is easy to eat, but it is useless if not eaten. It will not do any good if we just stare at the loaf. Just as we have to *eat* bread for it to do us any good, so we have to come personally to Jesus believing that He loved us and died for us, and ask Him to forgive us and make us His children. It is just as useless to come to Sunday School and learn about the Lord Jesus if we never believe on Him and go to Him for salvation.

What about us? We have heard about two kinds of bread. Which will you spend your life working for? Teachers wishing to give an example of a man who was thoroughly dissatisfied with life, even though he had scored fame and success, and who described his greatest discovery as 'the Lord Jesus', could tell their class about James Simpson*, the discoverer of chloroform.

Some further lessons from bread

(1) Bread is a *basic* food. In olden times, before anything else was bought for the family's food, bread was acquired (or made). So, if anyone is to be a complete person, the Bread of Life (the Lord Jesus) must come before anything else. The search to find Him must be regarded as more important than our career, marriage, home, etc.

(2) Bread is necessary every day. Real Christians receive the help and blessing of the Saviour every single day. They pray, read God's Word, and so experience the unmistakable help of the Lord every day without exception.

(3) Bread builds up the body. There is protein in bread which is essential to make the body strong. People who draw on the Lord Jesus are built up in their understanding of God and of life, and develop deeper, stronger characters.

(4) Bread provides energy also. Christians are given by Christ happiness and great motivation for life. They receive strength to overcome temptation, to cope with life's stresses and strains, and to tell others about the Lord.

(5) Bread is comparatively cheap and suits everyone. Conversion to Christ is for all – rich or poor, wise or simple, old or young. The Bread of Life – the Lord – will receive and bless all who sincerely come to Him for pardon and life.

*For a brief life of James Simpson, see *Men of Destiny*, Peter Masters, pp 36-47.

Urge your class to turn to the Lord Jesus in the spirit of this verse:–

> *Thou art the Bread of Life,*
> *O Lord, to me,*
> *Thy holy Word the Truth*
> *That saveth me;*
> *Give me to eat and live*
> *With Thee above,*
> *Teach me to love Thy Truth,*
> *For Thou art love.*

The Light of the World (40)
The Man Born Blind

John 9.1-39

Aim: To help the children see that unless they have had their eyes opened by the Lord they are blind to the things which really matter. This lesson also affords a special opportunity to explain 'grace'.

Teachers' Introduction

Children today are programmed to believe only in what they can see. We have to convince them that there is a whole realm beyond the physical which is far more important. Sin has blinded every human being to these things, but we can lead them to the Light of the World. The way in which the Lord restored the blind man's sight is full of significance. It enables us to explain simply and clearly that our cure can only be effected by the grace and power of the Saviour. The way of salvation is still as free and straightforward as it was to the blind beggar. The experience of receiving sight is still as dramatic.

Lesson Outline

A riddle. We are often frightened without it. You cannot touch it, but your eyes cannot work without it. Many animals avoid it. What is it? (Light.)

Born blind. Describe this man who had been blind from birth. Encourage the children to think what it must be like never to have been able to see. Unlike a person who goes blind later in life, no one could describe things to him meaningfully. The man did not know what colour was, nor could he imagine distances or visualise what people looked like. He lived in constant danger, unable to see where he was going or what was coming towards him.

The Bible tells us that there is a sense in which everyone ever born is blind! Explain to the children that we are all blind spiritually. We do not know God, we cannot feel His presence or power. We do not know where to find Him so we cannot pray to Him or ask His guidance. We never experience His love and power. We are blind to our soul's danger. All these things belong to another world which we cannot begin to see. If someone were to describe them to us, it would be like trying to describe what dry land is like to a fish! The blind man was sitting close to Jesus, but he was not excited because he could not see Him. Before we are converted we see nothing of interest in the Saviour.

The effect of light. Help the children to see that when God first shines into our hearts, the things which we begin to see are not always pleasant.

(a) Use the picture chosen by Charles Kingsley in 'The Water Babies' of the filthy, dirty, little chimney-sweep who, looking for the first time into a mirror, was thoroughly frightened and terrified by his own reflection.

(b) Describe the glass lantern which is old but looks quaint and nice until someone puts a candle in it. Then the filthy cracks of the stained glass become apparent, and the appearance becomes horrible.

Describe what nice, pleasant people we imagine ourselves to be before we see ourselves in God's light. Then we suddenly realise with horror that our hearts are full of selfishness (we think only of ourselves and what we want). Our hearts are also full of pride (we have such cocky notions of our own achievements and very little respect for others), as well as deceit (we always see things the way we want to see them, not the way they really are), and uncleanness (we much prefer to take an interest in things which are rude and wrong than those which are good and wholesome). Like the blind man we need desperately to be healed and cleansed. How was he healed? How was he made to see?

The Lord Jesus (a) spat on the dry dirt, (b) made it into clay, (c) applied it to his eyes, (d) told him to 'go and wash'.

A simple thing. Jesus did a very simple, 'common' thing. He made clay from spittle and earth and put it on the man's eyes. What was He teaching us by this? Here are the lessons:–

(1) This proved that it was the Lord Jesus Who had healed the man. Earth and spittle are not capable of restoring sight to the blind person. Anyone can make clay like this, but it certainly will not make blind people see. In the spiritual realm too, we have to learn first that Jesus is the only person Who can remove our sins and make us see God. No other teacher or remedy has ever been successful.

(2) Clay made from earth and spittle is surely the cheapest medicine you would ever come across! No one has to pay for these ingredients, and we are reminded from this that when the Lord Jesus restores our spiritual sight He does so quite freely. His mercy is free. We cannot pay for or earn our salvation. It is entirely of grace.

(3) Remind the children that they probably would not enjoy having clay put on their eyes. The blind man might have preferred Jesus to do 'some great thing' – like Naaman of old – in order to procure his sight, but the Saviour chose very lowly and common means. Similarly, being converted is a very humbling experience. It means admitting our sin and shame; it means acknowledging our worthlessness; it means asking the Lord Jesus to give us pardon and forgiveness. Many people – even children – would prefer to do some hard thing like going through a ritualistic ceremony, or following a course of self-denial and good works. But if we want to receive spiritual sight we have to forget our pride, and humbly follow God's instructions.

Sent to the pool. Jesus took the initiative in healing the blind man. He found the man whom His Father had sent Him to heal. He made the clay and it was He Who anointed the man's eyes. But then He asked the blind man to do something. He sent him to the pool of Siloam to wash. What would have happened if he had delayed and decided to 'sleep on it'? Would the clay not have dried and cracked and fallen off?

Similarly, when the Lord Jesus comes to us and shows us the way of forgiveness, we must be ready, not only to repent and accept His Word, but also to obey His command urgently. We sometimes call this 'surrender'. We have to say, 'I will give Thee my life, my all, and obey.'

Sight. 'So I went away, and washed, and I received my sight,' said the man who had been blind. How simple, yet how effective! Help the children to imagine what it must have been like for this man to see for the first time. What would he have seen first? How pleased he must have been to see his parents. How overcome to look across the countryside and to see the sky, the trees, the hills.

Seeing the Lord. Then describe to the class in the most exciting and vivid way you know how what it is to have the eyes of your soul opened. Point out what it means to find and see the Lord Jesus as your own Saviour and Friend. Tell the class how you begin to realise that when He died on the cross, He did it for *you*, to take away *your* sins. Express the sense of love and wonder and gratitude which overwhelms you at that moment. The more you look, the more you see. In fact you could 'almost look your eyes away'.

Then explain that a Christian discovers a whole new world. When we are converted we are shown the point and purpose of life; no more aimless drifting through months and years! We are given a grand commission, which will motivate us through life, to bring others to the Light of the World. To our never-ending joy we are assured that we are now members of the royal family of Heaven, daily cared for by God Himself. We are promised that at the end of our earthly journey we will have a place kept for us in a city 'which has no need of the sun ... for the glory of God will lighten it and the Lord Jesus Himself is the light thereof' (*Revelation 21.23 AV*).

Ask the class if they have ever seen and understood these great things. The blind man never forgot the experience. From that moment onward, he would not hear a word spoken against Christ. He believed everything the Saviour told him and was soon to be found worshipping at His feet. Has this ever happened to you? Every Christian can say with the blind man, 'Whereas I was blind, now I see.' Why stay in the darkness any longer? The Lord Jesus is still the Light of the World. Without Him you face a dark life and an even darker death.

The Good Shepherd (41)
The Lord's Love for His People

John 10.1-18 (and Psalm 100.3)

Aim: To show the compassion of the Saviour and the way He calls people to Himself.

Teachers' Introduction

We have seen the work of the Lord pictured in terms of water, bread and light. Now we turn to the very human and tender concept of a shepherd. Incidentally we have here a good opportunity to counteract the 'image' given to the Lord by the world, which portrays Him as a soft person with a silky-smooth voice and a long white robe, suggesting a weak, unreal 'do-gooder'. One may well introduce the lesson by describing the work of an Eastern shepherd as being one of the toughest jobs imaginable.

These men lived out in the mountains in the biting cold and scorching heat. They were often kept awake most of the night. They trekked for miles with heavy packs such as even modern, highly-trained, professional soldiers are not required to carry. They daily defended the flock against wolves and other beasts. (For their own information teachers may like to see Jacob's description of a shepherd's work in *Genesis 31.38-40*.)

The picture of the shepherd is chosen for Christ because the shepherd was tough, courageous, resilient and capable above any other Eastern worker of those days. So the Son of God is powerful, resourceful and courageous above everyone else. Before we present Him as the all-loving Saviour and protector of souls, we must make it plain that firstly He is the all-powerful, all-knowing Creator God.

Furthermore, the picture of the shepherd is chosen for Christ because it shows two aspects of His wonderful character. Never forget that the shepherd who will trek miles to save lost sheep, bind their wounds and carry them home is the very same shepherd who will draw his sword and thrust it through a wolf.

The picture of a shepherd is chosen in Scripture partly to save us from making the mistake of presenting the tender love of Christ at the expense of His righteousness, justice and power. That is why, when we come to the tender call of the Shepherd, we must go on to speak of how God also commands and warns people everywhere to repent. The children must understand that the tender call is to save us from the certain alternative of coming judgement.

Lesson Outline

A riddle. You cannot see it but it is more important to you than anything you can see. Rich men would exchange their fortunes for it. You cannot measure it but it is one of the most powerful forces on earth. What is it? (Love.)

What is God like? (This point is particularly applicable for older classes.) Describe how people have always been curious about God. From earliest history until now in every country of the world people have wondered if there is an almighty God, and if so, what He is like. They have come up with all kinds of ideas. But of all the non-Christian religions (and these include Buddhism, Islam, Hinduism), there is none which tells us that God is love and that He is concerned to save each one of His creatures by an act of unearned, undeserved favour.

Christianity is different from every other religion because, instead of leaving us to imagine what God is like, it tells us of a *personal* God Who has spoken and revealed Himself. The Lord Jesus Christ was not just a man. The Bible teaches that He was a member of the Godhead and that He came to tell us all we need to know about the everlasting, Creator God.

In this chapter of John's Gospel we make the most remarkable discovery about God's nature. We are told by God's own Son that He is to be compared with a good shepherd. And when the Lord Jesus saw a great crowd of people *(Mark 6.34)*, He was filled with pity because He saw them as *sheep without a shepherd*.

If we can imagine what it is like for sheep to be without a shepherd, we shall see ourselves as Jesus sees us:–

Lost. Sheep need a shepherd, and they did so particularly in those days when wild beasts and sheep-thieves roamed Eastern countries. Without the shepherd all kinds of disasters occurred to the sheep. Just as sheep need a shepherd, so we need to know God. We were made by Him and we shall always be unhappy and dissatisfied until we return to Him. Our lives in this world will have no point or purpose, no sense of direction, because like sheep without a shepherd we are lost. We shall wander aimlessly through life; but even worse we shall be –

Hungry. The sheep depended on their shepherd to lead them to green pastures *(Psalm 23)*. They had no map or compass or understanding of the terrain, and without a shepherd, before long pangs of hunger would grip them. It is the same with us. Without the Lord we ourselves soon become weak and dissatisfied. We were meant to be fed daily by God with spiritual blessings. No wonder we are so restless without Him; but even worse we shall become –

Diseased. Imagine what happened to a sheep which developed some terrible disease, if it was miles away from the shepherd. Gradually its condition would worsen and pain would set in. If help was still not forthcoming it might die in agony. This too is a picture of us. We often tell you about the disease of sin, which untreated, affects every part of us more and more.

We may *seem* like innocent lambs to begin with but before long pride, conceit, greed and lies will be taking their toll and wrecking our character. Finally they will carry us to the grave and on into hell itself. How desperately we need the care and attention of a Shepherd. However, in addition to becoming diseased, we may be –

Injured. Sheep are said to be silly creatures at times. They can so easily go astray, miss their footing, fall and injure themselves. They need a shepherd to keep a watchful eye over them. For us too there are all sorts of tragedies and disasters to encounter in life. Perhaps some of these have already happened to you. Many children know what it is for a mother or father to leave the family. Some may have a parent who has died. There are children who are suddenly hit by illness or injury. It is at such times that we need the love and affection of a heavenly Shepherd. But even worse we are in danger of being –

Devoured. In Eastern countries sheep were constantly being hounded by wolves and other wild beasts. Sometimes a sheep-stealer would lure them away to certain death. Without a shepherd they were defenceless against such superior forces. They needed someone stronger and wiser to protect them against these enemies. Similarly, we are vulnerable to all kinds of people who seize us for their own advantage. They make all kinds of promises but they take far more from us than they give. How easily we are taken in by this world's promises!

How many young people set out into life, full of hope and optimism, only to be bitterly disappointed in middle life and old age! The Lord Jesus knows that these thieves not only injure us, but they steal us away from Him. If we follow them we may be forever lost, and sentenced to spend eternity lost and away from God.

The Good Shepherd. We have seen how much sheep need a shepherd. The Lord Jesus Christ described Himself as our Good Shepherd. If we belong to Him we shall discover for ourselves how great and good He is. Again let us learn from the shepherd picture:

(a) A good shepherd is dedicated to his sheep. Even today in England there are shepherds who spend their whole lives caring for sheep. Some were interviewed recently on television. They said they never took a holiday like other workers and seldom even spent a day away from their hills. The Lord Jesus Christ loves His people. He thought nothing of leaving His home in Heaven to come and live in our poor world. There was nothing He would not do to help and guide and rescue His 'lambs'.

(b) Sometimes when wild animals attacked, the shepherd had to be prepared to risk his life in order to protect his sheep. The hired shepherd soon disappeared when danger was imminent, but the true shepherd would do anything to save his flock. Even so, the Lord Jesus was willing to give His life to save His people from sin. That was why He allowed evil men to hang Him on a cross, where He took all our sin and shame and died for us. Only He could rescue us from sin and death and hell, and He did it willingly because He loved His people.

The shepherd's call. We have heard about the sheep needing the shepherd and we have learned what a good shepherd does. But how could lost sheep find their shepherd? How could they return when they were so lost and so wounded? The answer is that they could not. Instead the shepherd had to search for them *(Luke 15.4)*. Likewise Jesus has to find us. When we are far away from Him – we may even have forgotten Him completely – He comes and calls us.

Imagine a sheep lying on a rugged cliff, terrified of a wolf's attack. The wind may have been howling and rain pouring down, but amidst all the turmoil the sheep would be quick to hear the voice of its shepherd, just as children recognise a parent's call, however much noise is going on around them. The sheep know his voice and follow him to safety.

When people become Christians, they hear the Saviour calling them personally. They do not become converted automatically because they attend Sunday School, or because their family are Christians. They respond personally to the call of Jesus. Once we answer the call of the Lord Jesus and repent of our sins, believing that He has died for us, then we shall come to know Him and experience His friendship and power. We shall want to please Him and to be with Him always, and we shall be anxious that other people who are lost should find Him, as we did.

Life abundant. Once a lost sheep was rescued it began to enjoy life as never before. It became well fed, protected and happy, knowing the daily care and guidance of the shepherd.

If you are made a Christian by the Lord, it will be the same for you. Far from the Christian life being narrow, cramped and outdated, as some people think, you will discover that you never knew real life before. You will find much greater happiness and fulfilment, much better friends and pleasures, much more knowledge and strength. Above all you will treasure the daily experience of walking and following the Lord Jesus Who loved you and died for you. He will be your Shepherd, your guide, your friend. He will never leave you nor forsake you and one day He will put you on His shoulder and take you to His heavenly home (*Luke 15.5-6*).

Did you ever realise that you were lost? Did you know that you have a Good Shepherd? Have you ever obeyed His call? What will you do without Him when life gets harder, when death is close? Answer His call now and you will never regret it; and He and the angels in Heaven will rejoice.

The Resurrection and the Life (42)
Jesus Raises Lazarus – Escape from Death

John 11.1-46; 1 Corinthians 15.50-57

Aim: To inform the children about death – its origin, its course and the only way of escape from it. To contrast the death of the believer with that of the worldling.

Teachers' Introduction

In days gone by, we are told, children were frightened into Christianity by threats of hell fire. As a reaction against this approach many Sunday Schools dropped the subject of death and hell altogether. This, of course, is equally wrong because of the tremendous importance of the matter, with all its eternal consequences.

We are fortunate, in one way, because as a result of the neglect of this subject, the children will be full of curiosity about what we have to tell them. As we teach them what the Lord Jesus Christ revealed on this subject, though we may see no immediate response, we may be sure that a strong impression will continue with them through life. Who knows but that some – even on their deathbed – may recall the words of a Sunday School teacher and seek the Lord's resurrecting power. However, we pray and long that they may find Him sooner.

Younger classes will probably want to concentrate on the events surrounding the miracle at Bethany, drawing simple but all-important lessons. Older classes should focus on the subject of death and life, and use the miracle as Jesus used it, to illustrate His great power.

Lesson Outline

A riddle. Show the children two similar objects (perhaps plants), one dead, one living. Encourage them to puzzle out the difference. What is the mysterious force which we call life?

What is death? What happens to us when we die? Is death the end? Does our conscious existence come to an end at the same time as our hearts stop beating? Explain to the class that many people think it does. Others are a little more thoughtful. They cannot believe that the *real person* comes to an abrupt end just because the heart and brain have stopped functioning.

As so many people have ceased believing in God, they have very little to say about death. It is an embarrassing subject for such people. As soon as death looks near, a dying person is whisked off to hospital, and apart from a few hours at the funeral, people try to forget that death is a constant and certain visitor. Only people who believe the Bible are clear about what it is, and what happens afterward. We are going to learn about this today. We can assure you that far from being a morbid lesson, it will be one of the most interesting and important of all.

Where did death come from? In the beginning God breathed into the first man a living soul, which was not meant to die. Remember how God warned the first man – *for in the day that you eat from it you shall surely die (Genesis 2.17)*. Only if man disobeyed would he experience death. Paul puts it plainly in *Romans 6.23: The wages of sin is death.*

Explain to the class that death is caused by sin. (Just as a tiny speck of rust heralds the eventual collapse of a car, so sin begins the inevitable rot which leads to death.) Adam's soul died the day he sinned, and his close contact with God was ended. Also, the ageing process began in his physical body. All the descendants of Adam – all mankind – because they are a race disobedient to God, are now affected by death. Our bodies deteriorate and die, and our souls are cut off from God, their source of spiritual life and power.

What happens after death? The Bible tells us, *It is appointed for men to die once and after this comes judgment (Hebrews 9.27)*. God is absolutely fair. He is no respecter of persons; He has no 'favourites'. He does not allow people into Heaven just because they are rich or famous, or even because they have been outwardly religious. We shall be examined by God's laws – those written for us in the Bible and those written in our consciences *(Romans 2.12)*. Nor is God like earthly judges who know nothing about the person in the dock, and can only take the evidence presented by others. God knows all about us. He knows every secret thought and He will open 'the books' in which our every action is recorded.

In our heart of hearts we all know the verdict, *There is none righteous* [good enough for Heaven], *not even one (Romans 3.10)*. We have all broken God's laws, and we have done so wilfully and deliberately. Not only this, but we have spurned God's offer of forgiveness and love. Those who are found in this position must be sentenced to the punishment and consequences of their sin in hell forever. Older classes might like to use the illustration of the driving test:–

(1) To make the test as fair as possible, the examiner is not left to his own opinion of your driving but has to mark a whole sheet, intended to test each motoring ability, eg: braking, use of gears, road sense, etc. In the same way God judges us by laws; there is no favouritism.

(2) If the examinee fails to reach the correct standard, he or she is not allowed a licence, not because the examiner is being spiteful, but because it would endanger that person's life as well as the lives of other road users if permitted to drive when unable to control a car. God does not want to shut anyone out of Heaven, but if we are laden with unforgiven sin, He has no alternative. Heaven would be Heaven no longer if He allowed us in.

Escape? Will everyone go to hell then, or is there a way of escape? We look for hope to the amazing account of what happened in Bethany – a village only a few miles out of Jerusalem.

(a) Describe how Lazarus – a close friend of Jesus – was very ill, and yet Jesus did not rush to cure him as his sisters had hoped. Why did He not go? Why did He allow Lazarus to die? See v 15.

(b) Describe how Jesus was touched by grief and sorrow. The Bible describes death as the *last enemy (1 Corinthians 15.26)*, and Jesus fully entered into the sorrow, the finality and the apparent hopelessness which surrounds death as He shared the grief of Mary and Martha. Invite the younger children (who may never have experienced grief) to imagine how sad Mary and Martha must have been.

(c) Point out – for the sake of the cynic – that there was no doubt about Lazarus being dead. He had been dead four days and showed the signs of it! Many Jews who did not believe in Jesus were present to witness these events.

(d) Tell how the Lord demonstrated His power even over death. He made His great claim – *I am the resurrection and the life* – and then proceeded to prove this to be so. We may have heard of faith-healers who claim to cure people of disease, but besides the Lord Jesus the world has never seen anyone who could raise people from the dead. (This was the fourth recorded person whom Jesus raised.)

A picture for us. The Lord Jesus had raised Lazarus' physical body, which was an unspeakable joy for his friends, and He did it to show what He could do for all those who believe in Him. When our bodies die, the Lord Jesus Christ will raise us up to live for ever with God in Heaven. If that is all death leads to, we need not fear it. In fact we can look forward to being with Christ, *which is far better*. As it says in *1 Corinthians 15.55 (AV)*, *O death, where is thy sting? O grave, where is thy victory?* We need not fear wasps that cannot sting!

Jesus here described death as a sleep. Sleep puts an end to all our fears and refreshes us for the next day. Believers die to the world and awaken to Heaven. Some teachers may like to use the biblical picture taken up by Bunyan in *Pilgrim's Progress* of crossing the Jordan before reaching the Promised Land.

New life now. But we do not have to wait for death to know and live with the Lord. Immediately we believe on Him and part company with sin, He gives us eternal life. Our sins are forgiven and we can turn to God and know Him day by day. We can begin to experience life as God meant it to be, before sin came into the world.

How? How can this be? We know that death follows sin. Every sinner must suffer death. But the Lord Jesus, Who was absolutely pure and sinless, went willingly to die on Calvary's Cross for us, to bear the punishment of our sins.

He did so because He loved us and wanted to save us from everlasting death.

When they laid His body in the tomb, it did not stay there for long. Death had no power over the Lord Jesus because He was sinless. It could not hold Him and so He broke free from its power and rose again. All those who believe in Him are freed from the power of death too, *that as Christ was raised from the dead . . . so we too might walk in newness of life (Romans 6.4).*

Application

Is this not the best news in the world? When people hear deep in their hearts (as Lazarus did) the voice of the Saviour say, 'Come forth!' then they find that they can leave their spiritual 'deadness' (cut off from God) and enter into a new life. Just as Lazarus could hear the voice of Christ *even though he was dead,* so we may hear the wonderful command of Christ (in the Gospel message) saying – 'Repent, and come forth from the grave of your present life!' When we really do hear the Saviour we obey Him, and then there is no need to fear death.

Has the Lord Jesus Christ ever raised you 'from the dead'? Have you been born again? Do you know God? Are you frightened to die? Or do you know the Lord Jesus Who is the Resurrection and the Life? He died to give you life. Have you ever been to the Cross, confessed your sin to Him and asked Him to raise you up? If not, do it urgently. No one knows how long this present life will last, but we know that just as life is short, so eternity is long. Do not risk entering it without a Saviour.

The Way, the Truth and the Life (43)
Heaven and How To Get There

John 14.1-14

Aim: To show the children that Heaven is far better than they ever dreamed, and to show them the only way there.

Teachers' Introduction

Heaven is another subject which, if properly described, will fascinate the children. If we allow the world to educate our children on this subject we should not be surprised if few have any real desire to go there. Artists, in particular, have left a very distorted and inadequate picture in most of our minds. We have the privilege of conveying some of the great Bible concepts to our class. Finally we return to our title to show simply (without confusing digressions) that there is only one way to Heaven – and that is through the Lord Jesus Christ. How concerned are we that none of the members of our class shall be left out? Now is the time for real concern and persuasion. Next week, even, may prove to be too late.

Lesson Outline

A riddle. There is a place so famous that all your friends will have heard of it, yet it is not on any map. Millions of people have gone there, and seen its staggering beauty, but no travel agent can arrange for you to visit. You cannot get there by air, sea, rail or road. Where is it? (Heaven.)

Raised, changed, glorified. Ask the children to imagine the death of a Christian. Suddenly or gradually this person sinks to the point of death, his eyes close for the last time in this world, but then, suddenly, the light of the next world comes on and he begins a whole new life; a great adventure.

(1) Think of the chrysalis which for months clings unnoticed to a twig as a dark, ugly lump. Suddenly a butterfly struggles out and is free to fly into the air and discover a new life in its beautiful new body.

(2) Or consider a giraffe in a zoo, cramped in a narrow cage, suddenly released into its natural habitat, able to run across the grasslands at enormous speeds.

Help the children to understand that Christians at death are raised above this world of flesh and time. They are set free from the narrow restrictions which have confined them to their earthly bodies. Not only are they free to explore the universe but entirely new scenery comes into view. Their wondering eyes begin to view another world which belongs to God and has been especially prepared for His people.

Heaven. Comment on the fact that people think of Heaven as nothing more than a kind of mysterious experience; a blissful state in which disembodied spirits rest, but which has no substance or shape. The Lord Jesus Christ spoke of

Heaven as a 'place', and the Bible tells us that it is a very real and certain place. It is as real and touchable as this world, but a million times more wonderful. Of course it is hard for us to imagine what it is like. Just as a person from a hot country finds it hard to visualise snow, so we who have only known earthly things find it hard to imagine Heaven. God, in His Word, has to use pictures which we can understand. Here are some:–

A city. In the book of *Revelation* Heaven is described as a 'city' with 'gates' (*Revelation 22.14*). Not the dirty, grubby cities we are familiar with today, but a magnificent city whose architect and builder is God (*Hebrews 11.10.*) Imagine a city not built with bricks, stones and concrete and shrouded with dust and grime, but built where the atmosphere is pure and invigorating. This city is full of light and surrounded with impenetrable walls to protect from anything which might pollute and spoil it.

Imagine spectacular ice-glacier valleys formed into amazingly beautiful buildings. Or picture steep walls as though they were hewn from gigantic, priceless stones and metals, like pure gold, jasper, sapphire, emerald and amethyst, interrupted only with gates of pearl. Instead of riding down uncleaned, crowded roads, imagine streets built of gold so pure that they shine like transparent glass. This amazing city has no need of artificial lights – not even the sun – for God's light forever shines in it. Imagine all the most exotic species of flowers, trees and plants – plus other even more breathtaking sights – crowded into the landscape. This may be a poor description of somewhere too marvellous for human words, but it helps us to understand something of the wonder of this city.

A home. The Lord Jesus Christ told His disciples that He was going to prepare a place for them in His Father's house (*John 14.2*). He used the word which meant not just a house with walls and a roof, but the word which signified a home. Suggest some of the features of a real 'home' – a place where you belong, where you are loved, where you can really relax and rest, and where you have hobbies and so on. Christians know that they do not belong to this world. The things and the people they love are elsewhere and they look forward to going home – to Heaven. There is no shortage of space there. Jesus says in our passage that there are many dwelling places in Heaven. He waits to welcome millions upon millions into His Father's house.

God is there. Illustration – here on earth we can only glance briefly at the sun and feel its rays. We dare not gaze at it or examine its features with unprotected eyes or we would be blinded. Similarly we cannot see God or begin to comprehend His greatness and glory with mortal, sinful eyes, but in Heaven we shall. There we shall not only see His throne – surrounded by His servants – but we shall see His face. Here on earth Moses had to hide from God in a great cleft of rock, for no one can see God and live, but in Heaven we shall see Him as He is, because we shall have become like Him. How full of unspeakable joy Christians will be to see the Lord Jesus, Who previously they had loved but never seen. Imagine meeting a person who had given his life for you; then think how much better it will be for Christians to meet their Saviour!

Refer younger classes to Midlane's beautiful hymn either in the lesson, or at some other point in the proceedings:–

> *There's a Friend for little children*
> *Above the bright, blue sky,*
> *A Friend Who never changes,*
> *Whose love will never die;*
> *Unlike our friends by nature,*
> *Who change with changing years,*
> *This Friend is always worthy*
> *The precious name He bears.*

A new government, new laws. Our world is governed by the law of sin and death. Even the best things in life are quickly spoiled and finished. Teachers with older children could devise a way of expressing the law of sin and death which is obviously at work around us. Teachers can pick out items appropriate for their classes from the following.

Flowers, so perfectly designed and so much to be enjoyed, fade and fall within days. Friends who like us often leave us for someone else and even turn against us (this is particularly true of under-elevens). Splendid meals are quickly eaten leaving a pile of washing-up. The job we have wanted and worked towards turns out to be a drudge and a bore. A bride is overwhelmingly happy on her wedding day but unhappiness and hostility surface before very long. Those people who do enjoy a happy marriage are parted all too quickly by death.

In Heaven these laws do not operate. Sin is banished, so the flowers do not fade, friends do not fail, work is always creative and satisfying, sorrow, pain and death are unknown. All the wrong and unfairness of earthly days will be reversed.

New friends. Children know only too well that everyone has their heroes. All of us can think of a great or famous person we should like to meet. Think then of Heaven where we shall have the privilege of meeting every believer from the beginning of time to its close, of every race and nationality. Imagine meeting Paul, who was beaten, shipwrecked, stoned, imprisoned and maligned so often in order that people like ourselves might hear how to be saved; or Moses who led two million people across the wilderness without knowing how their daily provisions would be supplied.

Suggest that the children would like to meet children from other ages – some from the Bible like Samuel and David. What a privilege to meet children and teenagers who were martyred in centuries gone by, or some who live today in lands where they are parted from their Christian parents. This subject alone could fill our minds for eternity.

The Way to Heaven. Thomas wanted to know the way to Heaven, and after hearing about this wonderful home, we too should want to be certain. Only a fool would set off on a journey not knowing the way, without a map, or without seeking directions. Nobody travels to a foreign country and arrives at the customs desk without a passport. Yet Jesus warned there would be many who would die without any idea where they were going, or without any qualification for entering that amazing city. That is why the Lord answered Thomas' question so clearly by saying, *I am the way, and the truth, and the life; no one comes to the Father, but through Me.*

If our names are not in the Lord's Book of Life we shall not be admitted. If we have never had our sins forgiven by the Saviour we shall find the gates closed to us. It will be of no use looking to anyone else to let us in: 'He only could unlock the gate of Heaven and let us in.' But if we are one of those who have left all to follow Jesus on earth; if we already know Him as our Saviour, Friend and Lord, then He will welcome us into His home, to be with Him and His people forever.

Do not trust to your own wisdom or depend on guidance from others who have never been to Heaven themselves. On this all-important matter trust only in God's Son and He will show you the Way, the Truth and the Life.

The True Vine (44)
How Not To Waste Your Life
John 15, Galatians 5.19-23

Aim: To show how futile and unproductive the life of an unbeliever is. To demonstrate that this is the result of sin. To give examples of believers who, however lowly, have been used by the Lord, and whose lives have been really effective.

Teachers' Introduction

This chapter has much to teach the believer but it also offers a challenge to the unbeliever. Modern educationalists speak of the gifts and potential capabilities of children as powers to be 'drawn out'. The children themselves are sometimes encouraged to believe that they are all budding stars.

It is an age of enormous self-confidence and self-esteem and we must somehow bring the children down to earth and help them to see themselves as God sees them. They need to realise how short they are of those special qualities which God looks for within – humility, honesty, kindness, etc. They must face the fact that in forty or fifty years they will probably have achieved very little if they live away from God.

God's standards are very high, and the branch which does not bear fruit is to be taken away. Even young children can appreciate this principle and should be earnestly urged to turn to the Lord now so that they can be made 'clean' in Him, and abide in Him and bear much fruit as life proceeds.

In this lesson time is deliberately left to allow teachers to give real-life examples of Christians who were truly fruitful for the Lord. These can be used to challenge the children to measure themselves and their achievements (or ambitions) by standards not common in modern life. Our aim will be to shame them into seeing their need to be grafted into the true Vine.

Lesson Outline

A riddle. Teachers should have hidden in a box a bunch of grapes or some other fruit. The riddle for this week could go along these lines: it grows on a plant or tree. It should be juicy. The plant would be useless without it. What is it? (Fruit.)

The farmer. Describe the farmer who sows his seed or young plants. When he inspects his fields he wants to see healthy plants. What will he do if there has been no growth?

(1) The plant may be covered with disease or pests (teachers could perhaps show a leaf eaten by pests). The farmer will have to spray this with insecticide.

(2) If the keeper of a vineyard or orchard finds useless and diseased branches with no fruit on them, he will in due course cut them off.

(3) If he finds a branch broken off from the main plant, he will throw it away, for it cannot possibly produce fruit if it is not connected to the plant.

God. God has not put us in this world just to please ourselves but to please Him and carry out His commands. One day we shall all stand before His judgement throne and, like the farmer, He will look to see what fruit we have borne. What will we have to show Him? Will He be pleased with us? Will He be glad that He made us or will He be sorry? Will He look back across the record of our lives and see wasted, selfish years? Will He see hearts full of sin and disease? What will God do if we have nothing for Him?

If our lives are full of the disease of sin – like a plant with diseased leaves – then only the Lord Jesus Christ can make us clean because of what He has done on Calvary to secure forgiveness. Those who have been forgiven love Him greatly and live to please Him. Soon their lives begin to bear the fruit listed in *Galatians 5.22-23*.

However, the Bible warns us that if we do not turn to the

Lord, we shall be (in God's sight) a branch broken away from its stem, useless and fruitless to God. Jesus said the only people in this world who can please God are those who know Him, love Him, and get power and help from Him. He is the plant and we are the branches. Anyone who tries to 'bear fruit' without knowing Him will fail, and at the end of life, will be rejected by God.

If we know the forgiveness of the Lord, we must stay close to Him – abide in Him. We must pray to Him, read His Word, meet with His people. Then His power will come into us. Not only will our lives please Him, but He will enable us to do great things for Him. We shall be able to bring others to know the Lord. Our marriages, our homes, our careers, our families will all bring glory to our Saviour.

Some real examples. As suggested earlier, some examples from Christian biography will help make these points in a very practical way. Choose people who can easily be proved to have borne great fruit for the Lord, eg:–

(1) The apostle Paul – who first tried to live a life for God without being connected to Christ. He counted his early days of worldly success as rubbish and turned to the Lord. Describe how he was used to turn the world upside down, not only in his own generation but in the subsequent course of human history.

(2) William Wilberforce – an example of a highly privileged man who was wasting away his life at clubs and gambling boards. Describe how, after his conversion, he was used to give dignity and freedom to many people, particularly those who had been slaves. England and other countries around the world were changed, because his life was given to the Lord.

(3) Fred Charrington – born of the rich brewery family. Instead of living a life of luxury and ease at the expense and misery of others, he parted company with the family business and gave himself to preaching the Gospel and helping thousands of poor people struggling against economic depression in London's East End.

(4) Charles Haddon Spurgeon – an example of a young man who gave his life to the Lord, and whose 'harvest' was so huge it can hardly be grasped. Mention the thousands whose

lives were transformed through his preaching, the orphaned children who were welcomed into his Homes, the preachers who were trained, and the churches which were built.

(5) Many pioneer missionaries (many from humble origins) have gone on lonely missions to once backward lands and preached the Gospel to those who were living in fear and superstition. Describe the transformation as hospitals were built to care for the sick, schools established to enlighten the mind, and churches planted where thousands came to know forgiveness and peace.

Application

Warn the children against estimating their worth (as most people do) in terms of worldly gain, which must be left behind at death. Help them to face up to the fact that, like the fool of *Luke 12.16*, they have no true riches with which to impress God – qualities of character such as only Christ can give. As bankrupts they need to go to the Saviour Who alone can make them fruitful and rich in a real and lasting sense.

Visual Aid

Some teachers may be able to provide a grapevine, but for most a rose branch will help to illustrate the necessity of pruning and spraying. Pictures of various fruits marked with the fruit of the Spirit from *Galatians 5.22* will be useful.

The Lamb of God (45)
Our Need Of Forgiveness

John 1.29

Aim: The aim of this lesson is to go more deeply into the nature of sin. Four vital aspects of sin will be shown to the children – rebellion, lawbreaking, disease and enslavement or bondage.

Teachers' Introduction

One of the shortcomings of our materialistic generation is its ignorance about the nature of sin. People seldom feel ashamed of themselves, and hardly ever look within for faults. Previous generations have been far less haughty and self-confident. Before we turn our children to the Lamb of

God, the Saviour of the world, we shall need to show them how ugly sin is and how desperately they need the Saviour.

We can illustrate this lesson with the case of a rich, swaggering, Victorian bank-owner who enters his bank shouting orders, instructions and insults at the poor staff, and who is then informed that his business has collapsed overnight and that he has become a penniless pauper. The parallel is obvious. Most boys and girls are supremely self-confident, and blissfully unaware of their status in God's reckoning. We need to shake their tragically false notions before we can direct them to the Saviour.

Lesson Outline

A riddle. We are all affected by this. It has many forms. It is often hurtful to others and painful to us, yet we may enjoy it, and will not give it up. God hates it. (Sin.)

Introduction. John the Baptist one day pointed to the Lord Jesus and said, 'Look, there is the Lamb of God Who takes away the sin of the world.' 'What sin?' your class may ask. Sin is an old-fashioned word. Here are just four aspects of our sinfulness: We are –

(1) Rebels. Tell the class about a man who hired an expensive car. He signed the contract, agreed to the rules and drove away. As soon as he was away from the hire firm, he began to abuse the car, driving it roughly and far too fast, so that it became covered in dents and scratches.

He drove so dangerously that he was soon involved in an accident, and smashed other cars and property. But he drove on, and decided to keep the car as if it were his own. Do you think he got away with this behaviour for ever? One day the police caught up with him, confronted him with a summons for dangerous driving, and arrested him for stealing the car.

Who would like to be in his shoes? But the Bible tells us that we are in a similar position (*Malachi 3.2*). Our lives belong to God, not us. He has lent life to us. We live in His world and enjoy all His gifts. Yet we live as if there were no God, and as if we could live as we please. All may seem well now, but one day God will come to take back the life He gave us. He will want an account of all our deeds, and where will we stand then?

How will we explain to God Who made us that we have wasted away our lives on our own personal pleasures and enjoyments without a thought for Him? Our excuses will seem paper-thin. How desperately lonely we shall be. How much we shall wish we had believed in the Saviour. We are rebels against God, and the punishment for rebels is eternal death. This is only one aspect of our sin.

(2) **Guilty – lawbreakers.** The Bible describes an event at the end of the world, the day of judgement, when we shall all be judged by God's laws. God has plainly laid out these laws in His Word, in ten short, simple commands or statements. They are also written in our consciences.

Everyone knows that certain things are wrong, and so no one can plead ignorance. Just as examination time at school reveals the students who have done no work during the term, so the day of judgement will reveal how far we have fallen short of God's holy laws.

Ask your class how they will fare when God – from Whom we can hide no secrets – judges them by His laws? Who will be able to say they are without sin on that day? Use the illustration of a video recorder. Suppose someone had recorded everything you said or did and then played it back. How frightened, how embarrassed you would be! Yet God knows everything, our thoughts as well as our deeds.

(3) **Diseased with sin.** If we find it hard to see our need for a Saviour in terms of His laws, here is a third way in which sin affects us. Sin is like a disease. It begins in a small way and spreads to infect the whole person. Its outcome is death. The longer we live the more sin takes hold of us.

What wretched people we turn into. One thing is certain: no one infected with this 'disease' is allowed to enter Heaven. How much we need a spiritual doctor – the Saviour – to cure this terrible disease. As an illustration teachers can give the example of lying. This will enable us to demonstrate effectively the 'growing' nature of sin.

Either give an actual case, or suppose one, of a child or person who lies. Show how, early on, the person has a sense of guilt about this, and seeks to calm the voice of conscience by justifying the lie. Thus, that person begins to deceive himself or herself that the lie is all right. Show how one lie usually leads to another (covering-up, stealing, threatening, etc) in an effort to keep the real truth hidden.

This is a simple example of how one lie can grow into a string of wrong and evil. Explain that this is why sin is described as a disease, because it is progressive – getting worse like an illness, and increasingly weakening and dis-figuring the sinner. Soon the person is in the grip of sin: telling lies automatically; hopelessly proud; unable to control temper, and so on. While sin is *avoidable*, and we are therefore guilty before God, yet as time goes on it is also a disease which holds us in its power, and from which we must be healed. Human beings become warped and perverted by sinful habits and ways. Furthermore, sin is like an *infectious* disease, because our bad example infects others, specially friends, and one day our own children. Finally, of course, it is like a *fatal* disease, because it will bring about our eternal 'death', when we are sent away from the presence of God, in the day of judgement, unless we repent.

(4) Slaves of sin. The Bible tells us that we not only need a Saviour to set us free from the guilt of sin but also from its power. We often think we are free people, but the Bible tells us that we are slaves. A slave was a person who knew no freedom. Slaves were owned by their masters, and their lives, their time, and their living quarters were not their own. Help the children to see that *they too* are the slaves of sin, of fashion, of other people's opinions.

Just as people wanting to get free of alcohol or cigarettes discover they are helpless slaves of these things, so we, wanting to be rid of sin, find that we are its powerless slaves. Ask the children how many times they have wanted to be better and have made New Year resolutions, etc. But they have found them impossible to keep.

Sometimes we have even felt a desire to seek the Lord and to go His way, but we discover that we are chained to this world and its ways. Is there any way of escape? Will anyone rescue us from this terrible position?

In the old days slaves could be redeemed. A member of their family or a friend could pay a price and buy their freedom. The cost was high and few slaves ever found a redeemer. What ransom would be high enough to secure our release from Satan and from sin? The cost was this: the precious blood or life of the perfect Son of God. Would He be willing to pay such a price to free such a person as I?

The Lamb of God. When John the Baptist saw the Lord Jesus he immediately pointed to Him saying, 'This is the Lamb of God (the Saviour promised by God) Who has come to take away the sin of the world.' Help the class to see the all-surpassing significance of these words. The Lord Jesus had come into the world to save us, the very people who have *rebelled* against His Father, and to bring us back to God. He had come to suffer in the place of those found guilty of breaking God's holy laws. He had come as the only Person with a cure for the *disease* of sin, and as the only One willing and able to redeem us from the *slavery* of sin.

Just as the lambs of old were sacrificed for the sins of the people, so the Lord Jesus was to allow Himself to be nailed to the cross of Calvary in order that we might be saved and forgiven. We have seen in past weeks that He came to be the Light of the World, the Bread of Life, the True Vine, etc, but best of all He came to be the Lamb of God – to bear away the sin of all who put their trust in Him, from whatever land or nation they may come, and in whatever period of history they live.

Have you ever put your trust in the Saviour? Have you ever recognised your sinfulness and asked Him to take it away? Do you thank Him from the bottom of your heart for bearing the pain and penalty of all your sin? If not, think about it very carefully and ask Him to make these things real to you.

The Son of God (46)
Revision

These [things] have been written that you may believe that Jesus is the Christ, the Son of God; and that believing you may have life in His name (John 20.31).

Teachers' Introduction

We share the desire expressed here by the apostle John as we seek to summarise the aim and purpose of this lesson and of the entire series. Before we close this great Gospel, we want to draw together all the amazing claims of the Lord Jesus, prove beyond all doubt that He was the Son of God, and urge the children to turn to Him.

Lesson Outline

Remind the children of the following statements of the Lord Jesus. Older classes can be asked to fill in missing words.

Jesus said He was –

(1) The Living Water – *whoever drinks of the water that I shall give him shall never thirst (4.14).*

(2) The Bread of Life – *he who comes to Me shall not hunger (6.35).*

(3) The Light of the World – *he who follows Me shall not walk in the darkness, but shall have the light of life (8.12).*

(4) The Good Shepherd – *all who came before Me are thieves and robbers (10.8); the good shepherd lays down His life for the sheep (10.11).*

(5) The Resurrection and the Life – *he who believes in Me shall live even if he dies, and everyone who lives and believes in Me shall never die (11.25-26).*

(6) The Way, the Truth and the Life – *no one comes to the Father, but through Me (14.6).*

(7) The True Vine – *every branch in Me that does not bear fruit, He takes away; and every branch that bears fruit, He prunes it, that it may bear more fruit (15.2).*

John said that Jesus was –

(8) The Lamb of God – *who takes away the sin of the world (1.29).*

(9) The Son of God – *that believing you may have life in His name (20.31).*

Help the children to see what amazing claims these first eight are, and how they all go to prove the ninth. Emphasise the apostle's teaching that the whole point of the Lord Jesus' coming was that we might have life through His name. Remind the class that it is no use knowing the names of the Lord Jesus if they do not believe on Him. (The greatest doctor in the world could not save the lives of people who refused to take the medicine which alone could cure them.)

Contrast the greatness of the Lord Jesus Christ with His humility in being willing to come into our world so that we might receive all these gifts.

Ask questions which not only test the children's knowledge of the incidents covered in this series, but, more importantly, ask questions which reveal whether or not you have conveyed these great claims of the Lord to your class in a clear and practical way. How much have you altered their thinking and way of life? Possible example questions are as follows:–

(1) Jesus said He could give 'living water'. To whom was He speaking and where? People who cannot find water get very thirsty. What happens to those who live without the Lord Jesus?

(2) How many people received a meal of bread and fish from Jesus? Why did they chase after Him the following day? He told them to work for a different kind of bread. What was that? How long does ordinary bread last? How long does the gift of life, which Jesus gives, last?

(3) Why does the Bible describe our world as dark? What does it mean when it says we are blind? What is it that we cannot see? How did Jesus make the blind man see? How can He make us see the things which really matter?

(4) What happens when people die? Why can unforgiven sinners not go to Heaven? Who brought Lazarus back to life? What must we do to receive eternal life? Why is it that Christians are not afraid to die?

(5) Why is Jesus the only way to Heaven? What is Heaven like? How can we be sure of going there? Who is the only Person Who can wash away our sins and make us fit to see God?

(6) What does a farmer or gardener do to make sure his plants yield a good crop? If we want to please God what has to happen to us first? What kind of things does the Lord God look for in our lives? What will happen to us if He does not find them?

(7) Why do we need a Saviour? What is sin? Why was it necessary for the Lord Jesus to die in our place? Whom is He willing to forgive?

(8) What does it mean to believe? What difference would it make to a boy or girl in this class? How could you tell if someone had really repented? Why was God willing to do so much in order to save us?

Lessons for Life, books 1-4

Lessons for Life 1 is the first volume in a series of four books of Sunday School lessons designed to cover a four-year syllabus. Each book follows the same format, consisting of lessons which have proved successful in Sunday Schools over many years, now revised by the author. The contents of each book are as follows:

Lessons for Life 1 (lessons 1-46)

Miracles Demonstrating Jesus' Power (Mark's Gospel – Part I)
The Lord's saving power seen in His power over nature, death, the devil, human need and illness (5 lessons)

In the Beginning (Genesis – Part I)
The truth about God, creation and the Fall, with the earliest salvation testimonies (6 lessons)

Opposition to Jesus (Mark's Gospel – Part II)
Examples of key sins – prejudice, pride, hardness, hate, etc – seen in the Lord's opponents, and to be repented of by all (6 lessons)

Highlights from the Conversion and Preaching Journeys of Paul (Acts – Part I)
Evangelistic lessons from the life (and converts) of the apostle (8 lessons)

God's Great Plans (Genesis – Part II)
Character studies from Abraham to Joseph showing the power and goodness of God towards His people (12 lessons)

The 'I AM' Sayings of the Lord Jesus (John's Gospel)
Exalting the Saviour through His own great metaphors – the Living Water, the Bread of Life, etc (9 lessons)

Lessons for Life 2 (lessons 47-92)

The Christian Pilgrimage – Salvation from Sin's Slavery (Exodus – Joshua – Part I)
The journey from Egypt to Sinai (8 lessons)

People Who Followed Jesus (Luke's Gospel – Part I)
Christian conversion and its chief characteristics (11 lessons)

The Christian Pilgrimage – Pictures of Salvation and Heaven (Exodus – Joshua – Part II)
The journey continues from Sinai to Jordan (6 lessons)

Gospel Appeals in the Saviour's Parables (Luke's Gospel – Part II)

Teaching the consequences of sin and the only way of escape (11 lessons)

Judgement and Deliverance (Joshua – 1 Samuel)
Examples and warnings for all, from Rahab to Saul (10 lessons)

Lessons for Life 3 (lessons 93-138)

Gains and Losses in Following Jesus (Mark's Gospel – Part III)
Repentance, faith and conversion, and their alternatives (8 lessons)

Great Differences (1 Samuel – 2 Chronicles)
Contrasts drawn from the lives of David and Solomon to illustrate conversion and the believer's privileges (12 lessons)

Early Reactions to the Apostles' Message (Acts – Part II)
Various categories of hearer and the Holy Spirit's work in their lives (6 lessons)

Sin and Its Cure (1 and 2 Kings – Elijah and Elisha)
The nature of sin and its punishment, with God's remedy graphically presented (8 lessons)

The Saviour Comes and Begins His Work (Matthew's Gospel – Part I)
A chronological account of the life and teaching of the Lord, highlighting His attributes and saving purpose (12 lessons)

Lessons for Life 4 (lessons 139-184)

The Word of God (The Division of the Kingdom to the Exile)
The Bible authenticated in history and in transformed lives (11 lessons)

The Life, Death and Resurrection of the Lord Jesus Christ (Matthew's Gospel – Part II)
Continuing the chronological account of the life and teaching of the Lord (10 lessons)

Character Studies from Daniel and Nehemiah
The transforming work of grace and its dramatic results (9 lessons)

The Ten Commandments
The 'schoolmaster' to lead us to Christ and the way of safety and fulfilment (11 lessons)

How God Fits Us for Heaven
The steps of salvation explained from Romans and other epistles and applied to young people today (5 lessons)